Springer Series on Social Work

Albert R. Roberts, D.S.W., Series Editor

School of Social Work, Indiana University, Indianapolis

Advisory Board: Joseph D. Anderson, D.S.W., Barbara Berkman, D.S.W., Paul H. Ephross, Ph.D., Sheldon R. Gelman, Ph.D., Nancy A. Humphreys, D.S.W., Sheldon Siegel, Ph.D., and Julia Watkins, Ph.D.

Risha W. Levinson, D.S.W., Professor of Social Policy and Director of the Service Development Division at the Adelphi University School of Social Work in Garden City, New York, holds a doctorate in social welfare from the Columbia University School of Social Work and a master's degree in social service administration from the University of Chicago. Dr. Levinson has delivered many papers at conferences, conducted seminars and workshops on Information and Referral (I&R), served as a consultant to the Veterans Administration and the Administration on Aging, and authored numerous articles and chapters in books related to practice issues and policy implications of I&R. Dr. Levinson's most recent publication is a volume on *Accessing Human Services: International Perspectives* (1984), which she co-edited with Dr. Karen S. Haynes. Dr. Levinson is currently Project Director of Senior Connections, a library-based interdisciplinary I&R model program that has been funded by the Administration on Aging and the New York State Legislature to train older volunteers and students from schools of library science and social work in I&R operations.

INFORMATION AND REFERRAL NETWORKS
Doorways to Human Services

Risha W. Levinson, D.S.W.

Springer Publishing Company
New York

Copyright © 1988 by Springer Publishing Company, Inc.

Springer Publishing Company, Inc.
536 Broadway
New York, NY 10012

88 89 90 91 **92** / 5 4 3 2 1

Library of Congress Cataloging-in-Publication Data

Levinson, Risha W.
  Information and referral networks.

  (Springer series on social work ; v. 10)
  Bibliography: p.
  Includes index.
  1. Social service—Information services—United
States.   2. Public welfare—Information services—
United States.   I. Title.   II. Series.   III. Title:
Human services.
HV29.82.U6L48   1987   361.3′07   87-9795
ISBN 0-8261-4820-4

Printed in the United States of America

To all my caring family—
who open new doorways for me that lead
to new explorations . . .

Contents

Part III Programming I&R: A Synergetic Process

Part IV Conclusions and Projections

Appendixes

Foreword

In view of the lack of planning of proliferating human services since the 1930s, access to essential services has become increasingly important. Certainly with the growth in public sector programs in the 1960s via the economic opportunity programs, and the expansion of information and referral (I&R) services in the 1970s through Title XX legislation, demands for I&R programs have increased, but not without attendant complexities and diversities. With the advent of the 1980s and the era of service cutbacks, I&R services have assumed even greater significance in efforts to maximize available resources.

The first serious interest in establishing I&R services in the United States as a universal service was the study reported by Alfred Kahn and associates in *Neighborhood Information Centers: A Study and Some Proposals* (1966). Yet, throughout the development of information and referral during the last two decades, no single publication has accurately documented the history, the structural and functional features, and the current as well as future projections of information and referral systems at the level of analysis that this present volume provides.

As Dr. Levinson herself notes, "all citizens in an industrialized society require human services to maintain a desirable standard of physical and social well-being, and the access to those services is and will continue to be via formal and organized I&R services." The necessity for formalized access services is a result not only of the complexity and proliferation of human services, but also of the barriers that have persisted in blocking access to needed resources.

The topical areas covered in this book encompass both historical and current trends in I&R development. Considerable attention is given to the impact of information technology, which has resulted in increased centralization of I&R systems concurrent with the decentralization of I&R service delivery. The author also introduces some timely and controversial issues on I&R advocacy programs, generic versus specialized services, and the significance of planning and evaluation in I&R operations. Her analysis of data utilization and collaborative strategies in the light of emerging megatrends suggests new and challenging directions for I&R networking.

This book should prove helpful to direct service practitioners and academicians alike. Providers and consumers of human services that operate generic and specialized services in traditional and nontraditional settings will find this book to be a useful guide in program development, staff training, and planning. It is to be hoped that this overview of the I&R experience in the United States will provide a springboard for ongoing research and experimentation.

It is paradoxical that while I&R is rapidly expanding and gaining recognition as an essential service, the literature in the field is relatively scanty. Indeed, this is not only a state-of-the-art book, but a definitive work in the limited but growing literature on information and referral. It is expected that this descriptive and analytical review of I&R will be a seminal work in the field of I&R. Dr. Levinson's extensive professional interest, knowledge, and experience in this area uniquely equip her to fill this void.

I have enthusiastically supported Dr. Levinson's efforts

throughout the various stages in the writing and completion of the manuscript. I am confident that this book will make a signifi-cant impact upon the further development of I&R access systems to human services.

KAREN S. HAYNES, PH.D.
President
Alliance of Information and Referral
    Systems, Inc.

Preface

A curious paradox has developed in American society. While social services have proliferated, bringing increased benefits to more population groups, the average citizen often experiences serious difficulties in reaching these services. The search for needed information and access to helping resources is particularly problematical for the economically disadvantaged, the sick, and the elderly.

A relatively new and expanding organized effort to overcome barriers to services and to facilitate access to existing resources has been the recent development of information and referral services (generally referred to as I&R). Since the emergence of I&R as an identifiable service in the early 1960s, a growing literature on it has begun to evolve; however, no comprehensive overview of the field reflecting the breadth and scope of I&R developments has previously existed. This book is an initial attempt to report on the rapidly expanding field of I&R that has emerged during the 25-year period from 1960 to 1985. The author's aim is to provide a systematic overview on I&R, a relatively new social invention that is designed to facilitate access to human services. Because of the recency and the diversity of the field of I&R, this effort may appear to be overambitious and subject to the hazards of overstatement or underreporting. Nevertheless, this book represents a first attempt at a comprehensive state-of-the-art report.

Viewing the phenomenon of I&R as a series of ongoing processes, the three major parts of the book deal with the developmental process in the emergence of I&R (Part I), the interactional process in I&R practice (Part II), and the synergetic process involved in the programming and networking aspects of I&R (Part III). Part IV concludes with a projection of major trends that suggest challenging directions for continued developments in I&R as universal doorways to human services.

The first chapter in Part I introduces I&R as an organized access system that is designed to facilitate entry to the complex maze of disjointed human services in a society in which services abound but access is often denied. While the evolution of I&R can be traced to the social service exchanges of a century ago, Chapter 2 focuses on the development of I&R in the United States during the past two-and-a-half decades, with some reference to other organized access systems abroad.

Part II, which examines the interactional process in I&R, begins with an analysis of the direct and indirect service components in I&R service delivery in Chapter 3 and suggests a structural typology of I&R organizations in Chapter 4. Given the impact of information technology and automation on I&R programs, Chapter 5 discusses the capabilities and potential of I&R in an information society. In Chapter 6, a discussion of staffing and training for I&R practice encompasses all levels of personnel, including professionals, paraprofessionals, and volunteers.

Part III deals with the synergetic processes of I&R programming and the diverse patterns of I&R networking. The identifiable developmental stages in programming are delineated in Chapter 7 and include the planning, initiation, operation, and evaluation of I&R programs. In Chapter 8, an analysis of diverse strategies for interorganizational networking is based on reports from selected networks of I&R systems. Part IV includes an assessment and projections of an expanding I&R movement in a rapidly changing information society that must be concerned with the human dimension in an era of technological advancement. Chapter 9 concludes with a series of megatrends that suggest changing directions and predictions for continued I&R developments that are aimed to facilitate access to human services.

To meet the apparent need for a basic reader on I&R, the text combines both conceptual aspects and empirical reports on I&R developments. Critical observations are introduced throughout the text to stimulate and challenge the reader to examine the multifaceted aspects of I&R. It is hoped that this initial effort will lead to further documentation, experimentation, and research.

Since all human service helpers seek to facilitate access to existing services, this book offers guidelines to service providers engaged in I&R and related human services. The content of the text is directed to social workers, teachers, nurses, and librarians, as well as to physicians, psychologists, therapists, and other helping professionals. To the large number of paraprofessionals and volunteers who are involved in I&R service delivery, the contents of this book may provide a knowledge base and a guide for I&R practice.

As academic courses in I&R programming continue to develop and in-service training programs in I&R agencies gain increased importance, this book may serve faculty and students, as well as staff members of I&R agencies, as an informational resource and an operational guide in the development and practice of I&R. For community leaders, agency board members, and social planners, reference to this book may provide direction in promoting and utilizing systematized entries to the vast array of human services. Since all persons are, at one time or another, users or potential consumers of I&R, the interested reader may find the contents of this book useful to become a better-informed citizen and an advocate for improved human services.

Acknowledgments

I express my gratitude to the many teachers, colleagues, practitioners, students, and friends who have been helpful to me over the past two decades in my studies in I&R. I am indeed most heavily indebted to my esteemed teacher and mentor, Dr. Alfred J. Kahn, Professor of Social Policy and Planning, who introduced me to the realities and implications of organized access systems during my doctoral studies at the Columbia University School of Social Work. I gratefully acknowledge the intellectual contributions to the field of I&R by Dr. Nicholas Long, who first ventured to conceptualize I&R theory and practice in his research reports and bibliographical compilations during the mid-1960s and early 1970s. While the emerging literature on I&R is still quite limited, a growing number of theorists, practitioners, and researchers have made significant contributions. I pay homage to this dedicated group of I&R experts and researchers by prefacing each of the nine chapters in this book with selective quotes from their respective writings.

My special appreciation to Dr. Harry Specht, Dean of the School of Social Welfare at the University of California at Berkeley, who encouraged me to undertake the writing of a basic book on I&R after he reviewed my manuscript for the chapter on "Information and Referral," which is included in the *Handbook of Social Services* (Gilbert & Specht, 1981).

I express thanks to Dr. Joseph L. Vigilante, former Dean of the Adelphi University School of Social Work, for his enthusiastic and sustained support of my interest in I&R and for his encouragement to implement innovative academic programs related to I&R education and professional training. My students have been especially helpful to me in their readiness and eagerness to participate in I&R program development and to explore new areas in I&R service provision. I owe special thanks to my colleagues, Professors Ralph Dolgoff, Gunther R. Geiss, and Narayan Viswanathan, and to doctoral students James Donovan, Beth Rosenthal, and Jacqueline Werner for their review of various sections of the manuscript. To Loriann Scerbo, graduate assistant, I express appreciation for her diligence and organizational skills in bibliographical research.

To Rita Edwards and Carolyn Schroeder, librarians of the Adelphi University Swirbul Library, I convey thanks for their assistance in conducting literature searches and providing me with supplementary materials. I express special appreciation to Carolyn Ann Thomas, word-processing specialist, and to my secretary, Catherine A. Bruder, for their skills and patience in producing neat and coherent copies of the text after laboring over more revised drafts of manuscripts than any one of us would care to remember. For their patience, support, and ready helpfulness, I thank editor Barbara Watkins and Dr. Albert R. Roberts, Social Work Series editor, of Springer Publishing Company.

To my colleague and associate, Dr. Karen S. Haynes, President of the National Alliance of Information and Referral Systems, Inc. (AIRS), I express my gratitude for her critical review of the original manuscript and for her insightful comments. For their assistance in supplying me with computer printouts and data analyses extracted from the 1984 AIRS Directory, I thank Jack

Parker of AIRS and Karen Geiss. Staff members of the United Way of America who have been helpful in supplying I&R data reports are Susan Mason and Dr. Douglas Warns. I acknowledge with special appreciation the professional assessments and thoughtful perspectives on I&R that Eva Nash, former staff member of the Administration on Aging, has shared with me over many years.

I am most grateful to my family for their consistent support and encouragement. As providers of human services in their own chosen professions, my children (Martin, Daniel, Judith, and Nancy) and their respective spouses (Katherine, Luna, Gregg, and Frank) have acknowledged and understood the importance of I&R and have lavished me with boundless enthusiasm in all my efforts. I reserve the most generous bouquet of thanks for my husband, Gerald, who never waivered from his absolute faith and confidence that this book would see the light of day.

List of Tables and Figures

Table

Figures

Acronyms

AAA	Area Agency on Aging
AARP	American Association of Retired Persons
AID	Accurate Information Desk
AIRS	Alliance of Information and Referral Systems, Inc.
ALA	American Library Association
AoA	Administration on Aging
APL/CAT	A Programming Language/Community Access Tool
AT&T	American Telephone and Telegraph Co., Inc.
CAB	Citizens Advice Bureau
CALL	Citizens Action Line Limitless
CAP	Community Action Programs
CASP	Comprehensive Annual Service Plan
CETA	Comprehensive Employment Training Act

CIP	Computerized Community Information Project
CRIB	Community Resource Information Bureau
CRIS	Community Resource Information System
CRT	Computer Remote Terminals
CUIC	Citizen's Urban Information Center
CWIS	Child Welfare Information System
DSS	Decision Support System
DIS	Direct Information Service
EAP	Employment Assistance Program
FIC	Federal Information Center
GAO	General Accounting Office (U.S.)
GPO	General Printing Office (U.S.)
HEW	Health, Education and Welfare (U.S. Dept. of)
HHS	Health and Human Services (U.S. Dept. of)
ICHR	Information Center of Hampton Roads
INTERSTUDY	Institute for Interdisciplinary Studies of the American Rehabilitation Foundation
I&R	Information and Referral
IRMA	Information and Referral Manual System
IRRS	Information Referral and Retrieval Service
LINC	Library Information Center
LSCA	Library Service and Construction Act
MEDASSIST	Medical Assistance
MIS	Management Information System
NACAB	National Association of Citizens Advice Bureau
NCLIS	National Commission on Library and Information Science
NEXUS	Network Exchange of Urban Services
NICs	Neighborhood Information Centers
OAA	Older Americans Act
OHDS	Office of Human Development Services
OMB	Office of Management and Budget (U.S.)

PIC	Public Information Center
RAP	Referral Agent Program
R&R	Resource and Referral
RSVP	Retired Senior Volunteer Program
RQ	Research Quarterly
SAIS	Service Agency Inventory System
SOR	Service Opening Registry
SSBG	Social Services Block Grant
SUAs	State Units on Aging
TIP	The Information Place
TTY	Teletype Services (for the deaf and hearing impaired)
UCFCA	United Community Funds and Councils of America
UWA	United Way of America
UWASIS	United Way of America Services Identification System
VA	Veterans Administration
VD	Hotline—Venereal Disease Hotline
VICs	Veterans Information Center
WIRE	Women's Information Referral and Education Service
WIS	Wisconsin I&R System

Emergence of I & R:
A Developmental
Process

1 Introduction: Access Systems to Human Services

"Access to information is a hallmark of the open society."
—Alfred J. Kahn, *Theory and Practice of Social Planning*

Not knowing where to turn for help is a serious problem in American society. The average citizen often incurs great difficulty in gaining access to needed services. Even finding information on where and how to qualify for benefits and entitlements is often a problem. Bureaucratic complexities, restricted admissions, extended waiting lists, and discriminatory practices often pose overwhelming barriers to those in need of services, particularly the poor, the ill, and the elderly. So complex and fragmented has the volume of services become that available resources are often unknown and difficult to reach.

Even when resources are located, extended waiting lists, exclusive eligibility requirements, and other barriers may obstruct access to services. The sheer process of application may in itself prove confusing and discouraging. Extensive and complicated application forms can be frustrating, particularly when the language is unclear and unfamiliar to the applicant. Registering a formal complaint or seeking legal redress for an apparent wrong or miscarriage of justice may prove to be overwhelming. Even the seemingly simple act of requesting help may engender feelings of stigma and inadequacy and may conflict with the American ethos of self-sufficiency and independence.

The literature is replete with accounts of serious consequences for the consumer that result from uncoordinated and discontinuous health and social services programs (Kahn, 1970; Hall, 1974; Aday & Andersen, 1975; Rehr, 1986). Existing services may be inadequate in quality, of insufficient quantity, or possibly too costly. Staff may favor selective clientele who fit the specific expertise of agency staff or who have a high potential of success. Access to services may also be hampered by class and cultural disparities between service providers and consumers that are often compounded by the provider's unfamiliarity with the language, customs, and cultural values of the I&R user. Persons with marginal incomes, even incomes slightly above the prevailing poverty line, are often automatically disqualified and denied Medicaid assistance with no recourse for appeal. The costs of deductibles and co-insurance payments for Medicare may be prohibitive. Other less apparent costs may be entailed, such as the expense of taking time off from a job to obtain services, the costs of transportation, and possibly babysitting charges. But over and beyond these fiscal costs are the social costs of deprivation and helplessness.

For those who are unable to overcome these service barriers, the consequences may be disappointment, frustration, and desperation. Many inquirers tend to be shunted from one agency to another, often subjected to a ping-pong process of repeated referrals and ultimately documented as "closed cases." Some never succeed in reaching a helping source due to any number of impediments, including language barriers, inconvenient hours of service, and remote distances. Not knowing where to turn, whom to contact, and how to proceed, these persons remain outcasts with no opportunity to link up with available resources (Milio, 1975).

I&R: RESPONSE TO A COMPLEX SERVICE SOCIETY

One organizational response to help people find answers to their questions and services for their needs is the development of information and referral services, generally referred to as I&R. During the past 25 years, from 1960 to 1985, I&R has evolved as a new phenomenon that aims to facilitate access to services. The emergence of I&R during the early 1960s closely paralleled the development of our "service society," in which services abound but access to them is limited. It has been estimated that two-thirds of our population currently derive their income through services and that by the year 2000, ninety percent of the workers in the United States will produce services and only ten percent will produce goods (McKnight, 1980, p. 15). In the realm of the social services, the expansion of social services during the last 25 years reflects enormous increases in the volume of services and the inclusion of larger numbers of beneficiaries within the broad spectrum of human services.

One of the expectations of a service economy is that the society will create adequate and appropriate services to meet human needs in response to the changing social, economic, and environmental conditions that create these needs. However, despite the development of a plethora of social services, barriers, fragmentation, and inadequacies persist. The reality is that our service society is overserviced but underserved. It has been noted that "the picture of social services in the United States is rather untidy; it contains numerous fragmented activities alongside overlapping provisions, all operating in jumbled networks of federal, state and local sponsors and regulations, implemented through various methods of professional practice" (Gilbert & Specht, 1981, p. 5). As new forms of social services have emerged and have been implemented, a comprehensive picture of the complex social services network in the United States is difficult to grasp. A complicated maze of social service programs with poorly coordinated policies and disjointed administrative structures hampers efforts to carry out service programs responsively and responsibly. Many different funding sources from the public and private sectors support similar programs, and variously organized service programs often serve the same or similar client groups. A bewildering array of constantly changing regulations, guidelines, and legislative mandates has added to the planlessness and disorganization of social welfare systems.

The development of I&R is in a sense a response to the complexity and unwieldiness that characterizes our service society. To inform the public of a readiness to be of prompt service, I&R organizations have identified their I&R programs with such declarative titles as *Call, Alert, Help,* and *Link.* In order to attract public interest, some I&R agencies use publicity slogans that ask *got a problem?, need an answer?,* and also employ attention-getting statements such as *We're the Good Lookers* or *We're Looking for Trouble.*

To date, there is no comprehensive inventory or unduplicated count of the total number of I&R programs, agencies, and networks that exist in the United States. Since the Brandeis national survey in 1967 (Bloksberg & Caso, 1967), various inventories have been reported by the United Way of America, by the Alliance of Information and Referral Systems, Inc. (AIRS), and by state and area Agencies on Aging published by the Administration on Aging (see Appendix A). However, these reports vary markedly, and the volume of I&R programs reported represents a gross undercount since a vast number of I&R departments and I&R units that operate within established host agencies are often not identified as I&R services. The growing volume of hot-lines, crisis intervention services, self-help groups, and I&R-related telephone services and information clearinghouses have not been systematically included in I&R inventories. A 1978 report from the United States General Accounting Office (USGAO, 1978) reported that the federal government spends more than 200 million dollars for information and referral activities. These expenditures are budgeted through at least 13 separate federal agencies and flow to thousands of individual I&R programs throughout the country (St. John, 1978). In the absence of a centralized, reliable inventory, it could roughly be estimated that as many as 10,000 I&R service programs and agency-based I&R services are currently in operation.

PURPOSES AND DEFINITIONS OF I&R

The term *information and referral* conveys many different meanings and interpretations. There is no single, universally accepted definition of I&R, nor is there a single model that represents an ideal or a typical service. It has been observed that "though access services are becoming increasingly important in complex urban societies, they are nonetheless among the least tangible of social services" (Gilbert & Specht, 1974, p. 121). Part of this ambiguity may be due to the lack of clarity in defining I&R within the total spectrum of human services.

The goal of I&R is to facilitate access to services and to overcome the many barriers that obstruct entry to needed resources. To realize this goal the purposes of I&R services may be defined as two-fold: (1) to link the inquirer with an available, appropriate, and acceptable service and (2) to utilize the data of an I&R reporting system for purposes of social planning, program development, outreach, advocacy, and evaluation. How these purposes are carried out depends upon how I&R is defined.

Various definitions and delineations of I&R have emphasized different aspects of I&R as a *service,* as an *organization,* and as a *network.* According to the United Way of America, "I&R is a service which informs, guides, directs and links people in need to the appropriate human service which alleviates or eliminates that need" (1980). I&R has also been defined as "an organization or part of an organization whose primary purpose is to link people and services" (United Way, 1980). I&R networks have historically been regarded as essential for effective operations on all levels. The development of an I&R community network was proposed as early as 1966 (Kahn, 1966). More recently, the I&R Task Force of the National Commission on Library and Information Science (1983) urged the development of "community I&R nets." Long (1972), on the other hand, was a strong proponent of state-operated I&R networks, as were Gargan (1980) and Garner and Haynes (1980). This concept of a statewide I&R network has gained strong support and has been implemented in selected states (Connecticut, Virginia, North Dakota). In view of the fragmentation and lack of coordinated I&R services, a recommendation for I&R networking on a federal level was proposed in a national survey of I&R conducted by the United States General Accounting Office (1978), which concluded that I&R is "a complex system that should be improved."

During the past two-and-a-half decades, the definition of I&R has broadened to include an array of service systems within vastly diversified organizational systems that have developed into ever-widening network systems. This developmental process in the evolution of I&R suggests that I&R can be viewed as a hierarchy of multidimensional systems that function as service systems, agency systems, and as networks of I&R systems. As noted on Figure 1-1, these I&R systems represent universal doorways to human services.

The underlying concept of I&R is the *system*, which is viewed as a set of interrelated, interactive components that function within defined boundaries or service areas in the environment in which the system operates. As a service system, I&R represents a continuum of functional service elements that range from information assistance, to counseling, to referral and follow-up. From a functional perspective, an I&R service system operates with the essential elements of clients, staff, and resources (input), all of which are involved in the service delivery process (throughput) that results in linking persons with needed resources (output). Based on the reported outcome of the services delivered (feedback), this cyclical process continues with new or modified inputs as the cycle repeats itself. A discussion of direct I&R services to clientele, and indirect I&R services in relation to policy, planning, and advocacy, is included in Chapter 3.

From a structural perspective, I&R represents an organizational system that may operate as an independent, free-standing agency, as an intra-agency system, or as a unit or department of a host agency (see Chapter 4). Operationally, it may be viewed as a network of multiple I&R systems that interact within the boundaries of a defined service area. For purposes of analysis, an I&R system may be regarded as either a centralized network that serves as the major generic system for multiple I&R systems or it may function as a decentralized network within which multiple I&R systems operate concurrently, though quite independently, with other I&R systems. An analysis of centralized and decentralized I&R networks is presented in Chapter 8.

Based on the multidimensional levels of I&R systems, the following two-pronged operational definition is suggested: *I&R is an organized set of systems of services, agencies, and/or networks that aims to facilitate universal access to human services. Through the use of an updated and readily retrievable resource file, trained I&R staff link inquirers in need of information and/or services to appropriate resources in accordance with acceptable standards of professional practice. Of equal importance to direct client services is the capacity of I&R to provide a reliable and retrievable data base for advocacy, policy, programming, and social planning in the interest of promoting and improving access to human services.*

DOORWAYS TO HUMAN SERVICES: A CONCEPTUAL FRAMEWORK

In viewing the voluminous and diversified range of human services, one might ask, "What is the role of I&R in linking persons to services and how broadly can human services be defined?" According to Kahn, the major fields of human services that have evolved pertain to health, housing, income maintenance, employment, and education. In addition to these five designated fields of services, a sixth field has been identified as the "personal social services." Specifically, personal social services consist of "programs made available by other than market criteria to assure a basic level of health-education-welfare provisions, to enhance communal living and individual functioning, *to facilitate access to services and institutions generally* (italics added) and to assist those in difficulty and need" (Kahn, 1969, p. 179).

As shown in Figure 1-1, the major responsibility for facilitating access and providing liaison to all fields of human services is assumed by information and referral operations within the field of personal social services. This graphic representation of I&R illustrates the centrality of I&R within the personal social services and

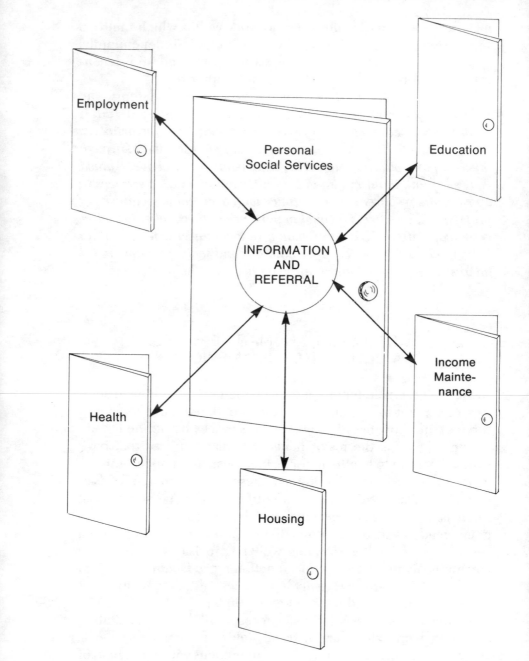

FIGURE 1-1 Information and referral: Doorways to human services

suggests the interrelatedness and interdependence of I&R as a major linkage system to all fields of human services.

As an organized access system, I&R represents a universal doorway for both consumers and providers of services. It is generally agreed that users or consumers are the primary and ultimate beneficiaries of an information and referral service. Experience has indicated that service providers are also in need of the capabilities of I&R to acquire up-to-date information on resources, to make appropriate referrals, and to utilize reported data from I&R operations for policy and planning purposes.

Included in the category of service providers is a broad array of helping professionals, paraprofessionals, and volunteers. Among the first-contact agents to whom people frequently turn for help with their problems are clergy, doctors, lawyers, and teachers, many of whom have need for information and referral services to carry out their professional and occupational service roles. Unaware of appropriate resources, community helpers tend to underutilize existing resources or overutilize those services with which they are most familiar. By linking up with existing I&R programs, service providers are able to expand their range of services, thus multiplying the effectiveness of their client services. Thus, for both providers and consumers, I&R offers an open doorway to the vastly complex and uncoordinated infrastructure of human services.

DIVERSITY, ADAPTABILITY, AND CHALLENGE

During the past quarter of a century, I&R has developed with great diversity and adaptability. I&R services operate under widely varied organizational auspices in both traditional social service agencies and in such nontraditional settings as public libraries, work sites, and shopping malls. Generic I&R programs that serve all inquirers and specialized programs that are targeted to certain age groups or problem-related areas are supported by many different sources of funding from the public, voluntary, and private sectors. Service delivery is conducted by varying levels of staff and may include combinations of professionals, paraprofessionals, and volunteers. The nature of I&R operations varies, depending upon whether the I&R organization is an autonomous agency or a department or unit within an established agency. I&R programs may range from an informal peer-operated hot-line to a highly sophisticated, multimillion-dollar computerized system. I&R may function as a telephone crisis intervention service or as a walk-in service. Organizationally, I&R may operate as a neighborhood agency, a municipal department, a regional network, a statewide system, or a federally mandated program. Because the settings and parameters of I&R systems are so varied in scope, in range of services, and in geographic service areas, an examination of I&R is an intriguing study in diversity.

The inherent diversity of I&R reflects its unique capacity to respond to current needs, opportunities, and prevailing trends with flexibility and adaptability. The impetus for the initiation of I&R services dates back to the consumerism and human-rights movement of the 1960s, when the social legislation of the Older Americans Act and the antipoverty programs of the Great Society provided new services and opportunities for the aging and economically disadvantaged. The continued growth of I&R in the 1970s also responded to new federal mandates, which explicitly recognized I&R as universal service (Title XX amendments of 1974), and thus permitted I&R to expand beyond the local neighborhood to include broader networks of I&R programs on regional, state, and federal levels.

Sensitive to demographic shifts and changing social needs, I&R is especially responsive to the multifaceted needs of a rapidly expanding older population. I&R has provided a point of entry into the complex social services systems with an immediacy that can handle crises and surmount existing barriers. In response to the multifaceted needs of an ever-changing society, I&R has sought to provide services to meet the urgent problems of child care, teenage pregnancy, drug dependency, unemployment, suicide, elder abuse, and other serious social concerns. While I&R has neither the sanction nor the leverage to solve major societal problems such as poverty, unemployment, and discrimination, it operates as a client-centered helping service and has proved to be an advocate for change, based on its capability to create valuable data bases for policy making and planning.

What has contributed to the tenacity and stability of I&R

developments is an extraordinary adaptability that has sought to maximize existing resources. Rather than creating new layers of bureaucracy, I&R programs have tended to develop within existing organizational structures and with optimal utilization of available resources. A case in point is the highly significant development of library-based I&R programs that have expanded the role of the library as a central information center as well as a highly suitable and accessible service center. Essentially, the development of I&R has involved minimal structural reorganization with maximal linkages between persons who need help and resources that can offer help. When budget cutbacks and service retrenchments were ushered in with the 1980s, I&R demonstrated its resourcefulness and pliability by creating interagency networks and new alliances that could pool resources and share centralized tasks.

The creation of widely diversified systems of I&R services, agencies, and networks has opened up new routes to access and new opportunities for innovation. The "network revolution" (Vallee, 1982) in this age of high technology and interactive information systems has brought about unprecedented capabilities for access to information that can be shared by larger groups of users. To what extent can I&R service providers use this new technology in service delivery systems to provide caring and sharing in a society of limited resources and boundless social needs? The enormous complexity of I&R that has resulted from its explosive and unchartered growth poses new choices and challenges. Is I&R a service in itself or only a first step into the service network? If I&R is viewed as a connecting link in a care-giving chain, who links the proliferating I&R programs? Is there a need for an "I&R on I&R"?

To assess the capacities, the potentials, and the constraints of I&R, an understanding of its evolution, as presented in the following chapter, is a logical beginning.

2 Overview of I&R: Historical Perspectives

"I&R has served in varying degrees as a focus for innovation in service patterns, in impact on the client
group, in organizational structure, and in deploy-
ment of resources (time or money)."
—Thomas Childers, *Information and Referral:*
Public Libraries

The genesis of access services can conceivably be traced to the
origin of the human species. Had I&R services existed when Eve
"referred" Adam to the Tree of Knowledge, or had there been
other available information sources, the outcome for the human
race might have been quite different. While the processes of information sharing, advising, referring, and advocating are basic to
all human interactional processes, formally organized I&R sys-

tems, designed to facilitate entry to needed resources, are a relatively recent social invention of the 1960s. However, the origins of I&R can be traced to the service organizations of a century ago that developed in the United States and in Great Britain.

I&R-TYPE PROGRAMS BEFORE THE 1960s

An overview of the developments of I&R in the United States reveals an uneven and generally sporadic growth of I&R programs. Historically, the antecedents of I&R services were the Social Service Exchanges that were established by the Charity Organization Societies (COS) in the late nineteenth century. While the stated purpose of the exchanges was to facilitate communication among agencies in order to enhance service coordination, the intent was, in fact, to restrict access and prevent duplication of relief services. In the interest of avoiding duplication and inefficiency, the exchanges maintained a central index of names of all recipients of cash benefits and counseling services who were known to service agencies in the community. The dual objectives of the exchanges were to prevent duplication of charitable grants to welfare recipients and to protect donors against multiple and overlapping demands. In effect, the exchanges sought to restrain rather than facilitate access to existing services.

Social service exchanges were also established in the community welfare councils that began to evolve in the early twentieth century under the newly organized United Community Funds and Councils of America (UCFCA—renamed the United Way of America in 1970). Local United Way organizations in major urban communities began developing I&R services as early as 1921 (United Way, 1980). From the first community council, founded in Pittsburgh, Pennsylvania, in 1908, the number of exchanges in operation in the United States and Canada had grown to 320 by 1946; however, by April 1963, the number had dwindled to 97 due to a variety of reasons, including concern over confidentiality of client information and a decline in the use of the exchanges by social agencies. The *Directory of Social Service Exchanges*, published by the United Community Funds and Councils of America in 1969, reported 40 social service exchanges, only eight of which were also identified as information and referral centers. While the precise number of exchanges that were replaced by I&R programs is not known, there is clearly a historical link between the social service exchanges and the establishment of information and referral programs at the turn of the twentieth century. Guided by the United Way of America (formerly UCFCA), community health and welfare councils began to shift from client inventories to systematized files of community resources for direct I&R services to clients. These resource files, which served as the source of published community directories, were also used as a base for decision making on budgetary allocations and community planning.

British Citizens Advice Bureaux (CABs)

Important beginnings of information and referral services occurred during and after World War II in the United Kingdom and the United States. With the onset of Germany's bombing raids on Britain in 1939, Citizens Advice Bureaux (CABs) emerged throughout the United Kingdom under the central leadership of the National Association of Citizens Advice Bureaux in London (NACAB). During the early 1940s, Citizens Advice Bureaux were established in local communities throughout Britain and were staffed predominantly by volunteers. Throughout the war, the bureaus responded to emergency information needs related to bomb shelters, relocations, housing, and other wartime concerns. After the war, CABs remained as permanent, free-standing local service agencies available for information, advice, and advocacy (Brasnett, 1964). According to the 1983-1984 annual report of the National Association of Citizens Advice Bureaux, nearly 1,000 CABs are in operation throughout England, Wales, Scotland, and Northern Ireland.

In search of a model access system, Kahn and his associates studied the Citizens Advice Bureaux in 1966, with a view toward assessing their applicability to the American scene. The CAB model was extolled for its "non-sectarian, non-political, non-discriminatory and stigma-free" qualities (Kahn et al., 1966).

Concurrently, Zucker (1965) and Wittman (1966) heralded the CAB system as a service modality that should be implemented in the American social welfare system. But while these authorities agreed that the CAB experience represents a vital and dynamic model of an organized access system, replication of the British CAB model in the United States social services system seemed neither likely or possible. It was recommended that the United States should create its own access models through innovation and experimentation. (See Table 2-1 for a comparative analysis of the British CAB model and the American I&R model.)

American Veterans Information Centers (VICs)

America's respose to the aftermath of World War II was the creation of a unique, though short-lived, development of Community Advisory Centers, popularly known as Veterans Information Centers (VICs). These centers were designed to assist the returning veteran in his transition to civilian life. In 1946, more than 3,000 VIC centers were reported in operation under the auspices of the United States Department of Labor.

The primary purpose of VICs was to provide information to the veteran on all government benefits and community services, and to make appropriate referrals for additional help. By 1948, more than 20 federal, state, and municipal agencies participated in this program. The original plan was to restrict the service to a single contact, referring to an outside agency if additional service was needed. The exclusionary policy of services for veterans only and the single contact policy very likely contributed to the closing of the centers by 1949. Though of brief duration, the VICs represent a significant model in the early history of American I&R services (Kahn et al., 1966). The developmental trends in the emergence of I&R from 1960 to 1985 are analyzed in the remainder of this chapter.

THE 1960s—EMERGING I&R SERVICES

The Public Sector

I&R is essentially a product of the new social programs of the 1960s, when federal government initiatives promoted the delivery of social services at the local level in both the public and

TABLE 2-1 Comparative Analysis of the British CAB and the American I&R Models

Aspects: Access Systems	CAB Model	I&R Model
I. Organization		
Auspices	Local authority	Local, state, or national auspices
Governance	Hierarchical structure: local management committee, area committee, national association	Varied, depending on auspices and funding; may be autonomous or related to municipal, state, regional, and/or national levels
Funding	Primarily local funding; contributory funds from NACAB	Multiple funding sources; public, voluntary, proprietary
Centralization/ decentralization	Centralized functions assumed by the national association (NACAB), decentralized local CAB services	No national centralized network; decentralized I&R service may be part of a centralized system within a given service area
II. Delivery of Services		
Mode of entry	Primarily walk-in services	Primarily telephone services
Staffing	Predominantly volunteers	Mix of volunteers, paraprofessionals, and professionals
Training	Mandatory training	Optional training
Technology	Uniform Information System	No common language, diverse information systems
Generic/specialized services	Traditionally generic; trend toward specialized services	Traditionally specialized; trend toward generic services
Legal services	Volunteer solicitors (lawyers)	Lawyers not directly involved
III. Policy–Planning		
Policy	Participation in national policy	No national policy
Planning	Consultation to other agencies for planning, evaluation, and research	Limited planning, research, and consultation
Program development	Standards & criteria enforced	Suggested standards; no regulatory measures

Source: Levinson, R.W., & Haynes, K.S. (1984). *Accessing human services: International perspectives*, p. 18. Copyright © 1984 by Sage Publications, Inc. Reprinted by permission of Sage Publications, Inc.

voluntary sectors. Within the public sector, the federal government promoted legislation to develop locally based I&R programs
to facilitate access to community services for the chronically ill,
the mentally ill, and the elderly. Central information centers were
initially established in Chicago in 1944 to provide information on
community resources to physicians and the chronically ill. In
1949, the Commission on Chronic Disease was established to
document the mounting problem of chronic disease and the concerns of the long-term patient. Based on the Commission's
reports and the recommendations of the 1956 National Health
Forum for Homecare, the United States Public Health Service
was requested to intensify its information and referral efforts.
With the development of the Public Health Service Chronic Disease Program in the early 1960s, various information and referral
centers that operated under the United Way of America began to
include information resources on health and the aging (Long,
1973a).

Supported by funds authorized by the Community Health
Services and Facilities Act of 1961, grants were awarded to selected public and voluntary agencies to demonstrate new and improved methods of providing community health services outside
the hospital, especially for chronically ill and older persons.
Twenty-eight federal grants, specifically designed for information and referral over a six-year period of time, and ten additional
projects related to I&R were funded under this legislation
(Long, 1973a).

The passage of the Mental Retardation Facilities and Community Mental Health Centers Act of 1963 was a landmark in
mental health care that advocated the relocation of mental health
services from traditional state institutions to community-based
facilities. Title I of the act, entitled "Services and Facilities for the
Mentally Retarded and Persons with Other Developmental Disabilities," specified information and referral, follow-up, and
transportation as vital services. Title II stipulated that the comprehensive mental health center should coordinate its services
with other health and social service agencies and insure that persons receiving services within a given catchment area have *access*
to all health and social services.

The earliest and most extensive development of I&R services

in the United States concerned the elderly. Since the passage of the Older Americans Act in 1965, the Administration on Aging (AoA) has assumed a major leadership role in guiding the development and expansion of I&R. AoA is the only national agency with a federal mandate to establish I&R services in its local, regional, and state agencies. Title III of the Older Americans Act provided matching federal grants to state-approved projects designed to deliver I&R services. Under Title IV of the act, the Administration on Aging supported a variety of large-scale research projects and special studies on I&R programs that have had significant impact on I&R developments for the elderly as well as for all population groups. The 1973 amendments to the Older Americans Act strongly recommended networking of I&R with other community agencies to promote effective, coordinated services to older persons.

I&R services were also suggested for the poor and other disadvantaged groups in the various social programs of the 1960s. To meet the needs of the economically disadvantaged, Title II-A of the Economic Opportunity Act of 1964 created quasi-public community action programs (CAPs) for service delivery to the local poor. This legislation specified the provision of information and referral services, as well as transportation, outreach, follow-up legal services, and escort services. However, since the antipoverty programs were directed to the most economically deprived groups in the community, I&R tended to be restricted to the local community action programs for the poor. Nevertheless, the leaders in the antipoverty programs, who were strong advocates for consumer rights, called attention to the need for universal access, not just access for the economically disadvantaged, to community services.

One of the efforts that was intended to promote integration and to help alleviate fragmentation of federally funded categorical programs was the Model Cities Act, also referred to as the Demonstration Cities and Metropolitan Act of 1966. To achieve coordination at the local level and help applicants qualify for benefits and entitlements, neighborhood service centers were designated as entry points for service delivery. I&R was suggested as one of a series of services along with outreach, transportation, follow-up, and advocacy to help clients obtain benefits and reach services.

Other federal agencies that showed an interest in I&R during the 1960s were the Social Security Administration and the Department of Housing and Urban Development. Some efforts were made by the Social Security Administration to conduct studies in order to determine the extent and quality of I&R services in selected local offices. However, the role of the Social Security offices in local I&R developments has remained quite limited, possibly because Social Security is generally viewed as a centralized federal operation and because of its apparently over-burdened workloads (Abbott, 1979).

The Voluntary Sector

The establishment of I&R programs in national voluntary health organizations in the 1960s occurred concurrently with I&R developments in the public sector. The National Easter Seal Society for Crippled Children and Adults and the American Red Cross published national guidelines for the implementation of I&R programs in their local affiliates and designed training programs for staff to promote access to community services. In 1962, the National Easter Seal Society for Crippled Children and Adults began a self-study that concluded that I&R should be conducted by all affiliates of the national organization to help disabled persons live purposeful lives through the effective use of available resources. For those communities in which I&R centers were not already in operation, local Easter Seal chapters were encouraged to provide I&R services along with specialized services for the disabled.

As early as 1913, the American Red Cross had incorporated aspects of I&R services into its home care program for the sick and infirm. By 1918, Red Cross workers had begun to receive I&R training in information-giving, referral, and follow-up techniques in disaster-aid programs. Operationally, the American Red Cross has endorsed the principle of collaboration with other I&R programs that operate in health and social agencies for the purpose of facilitating access to services for the civilian population as well as for military personnel. Traditionally, the American Red Cross has responded with crisis intervention programs, including I&R-type services to provide emergency aid under catastrophic conditions (Tannenbaum, 1981).

In a joint effort to establish guidelines and basic criteria for the rapidly emerging I&R programs that began in the 1960s, Bloksberg and Caso (1967) conducted the first comprehensive national survey of I&R services under the co-sponsorship of the United States Public Health Service and the Florence Heller Graduate School for Advanced Studies in Social Welfare at Brandeis University. Out of a total of 269 information and referral centers that were included in the study, more than half of the centers (151) reported specialized I&R programs for the elderly and I&R services related to health and mental health problems, particularly alcoholism. The remaining I&R programs (118) identified their programs as generic. The survey findings emphasized the need for continued research and evaluation and anticipated the rapid expansion of I&R that occurred in the 1970s.

THE 1970s—GROWTH OF I&R AGENCIES

The 1970s marked a period of rapid growth of I&R service organizations. New free-standing I&R agencies emerged concurrently with I&R units and departments that developed within existing health and social service agencies. A mounting interest in universal service provision suggested the need for more generic I&R services. Consequently, broader population groups became the beneficiaries of I&R services, and I&R programs emerged in new and nontraditional settings.

In an effort to promote service integration through I&R at the federal level, a trial-balloon proposal was drafted in 1978 by the Office of Human Development. The bill proposed that an I&R system be established to facilitate access to the specific services that were designated under Title XX of the 1974 Social Security Act. Owing mainly to budgetary constraints, the proposal failed to receive approval from the Office of Management and Budget (OMB) and was therefore never submitted to Congress. The main reason given for OMB's refusal was the estimated high cost of $50 million to carry out the proposed program. However, even after the budget was reduced to $10 million, the proposal was rejected a second time in 1979, possibly due to other competing programs and the prevailing budget-cutting climate within the federal government. Therefore, this effort to promote the functional integration of services under Title XX legislation through I&R was thereby aborted (Tatara, 1979).

The 1970s was also a period of large-scale research projects that was sponsored by the Administration on Aging (AoA). In 1975, a study of applied management services, supported by AoA, reported the relative benefits and limitations of age-segregated versus age-integrated information and referral services. The general conclusion was that age-specific programs ultimately and inevitably require access to generic age-integrated I&R services. Another extensive study sponsored by AoA was the three-volume evaluation of I&R services by Mark Battle Associates (1977), which recommended greater availability and better accessibility of I&R services for the elderly.

During the five-year period from 1969 to 1974, the AoA also sponsored a series of working papers and research studies conducted by Dr. Nicholas Long of Interstudy Associates, a research organization located in Minneapolis. Long developed an extensive series of working papers published by Interstudy on specific skills and techniques involved in I&R program development and aspects of service delivery, including information-giving and referral (1971), interviewing (1974), follow-up (1971b), and reaching out (1973). Long's functional analysis of the 1967 survey by Bloksberg and Caso provided a valuable interpretation of the impact of I&R and highlighted the capability of I&R to serve as a valuable social planning resource (1971). An evaluative study of the Wisconsin I&R system (WIS), conducted by Long and his associates during the early 1970s, set a precedent for evaluative research in I&R networking (Long, 1973b). Under Long's leadership an extensive annotated bibliography on I&R was published in 1972 that reflected an early state-of-the-art report on I&R at that point in time (Bolch, Long, & Dewey, 1972).

The Expanding Role of the State

A historical benchmark in the shift toward universal I&R programs was the implementation of Title XX of the Social Security Act in 1974. The public provision of I&R for all citizens and not for the poor alone represented a major breakthrough in social welfare provision. The availability of Title XX funds for I&R program development and I&R training contributed to the rapid expansion of I&R services that far surpassed I&R developments prior to the 1970s and significantly expanded the role of the state in I&R programs.

According to reported data from the Comprehensive Annual Service Plans (CASP) submitted by each state, the number of I&R services funded under Title XX increased from 14 state programs in 1975 to 32 I&R programs in 1977. By 1981 almost all states reported some level of I&R services, although the actual amounts allocated by each state for I&R varied enormously. The expanded role of the state created a trend toward increased centralization of I&R systems at state and regional levels, concurrent with the trend toward decentralization of I&R service systems to promote local service delivery. One of the major goals of state-operated and state-supported I&R programs has been the development of uniform classification systems and standardized reporting procedures. Beginnings of statewide I&R systems were made by the Georgia Tie-Line and the Info-Line that developed in Connecticut during the early 1970s.

In the absence of uniform federal regulations and a common language for standardized reporting of services, many states that provided I&R under Title XX did not assign specific staff to I&R programs; nor were standards for the organization and delivery of I&R services clearly defined. Consequently, broad diversities and disparities in I&R programs were created between states. In view of the options offered under Title XX, some states chose not to operate their own I&R systems but to contract with I&R services that operated outside of the public sector. Thus an important precedent for public–voluntary partnerships in I&R service delivery was established.

Nontraditional Settings

The expansion of I&R in the 1970s occurred not only within traditional social agencies but also extended to nontraditional settings, such as public libraries and the work place. The informational role of the library was extended whereby the public library could serve both as a local information center and a direct service center. The earliest experiment in library-based I&R programs was conducted in 1969, when the Enoch Pratt Free Library Service in Baltimore collaborated with the Library School at the University of Maryland to operate the Public Information Center (PIC). In spite of its limitations, due to inadequate staff and insufficient top-level administrative support, PIC set a notable precedent of a library-based I&R service until its close in 1973 (Donahue, 1976). Unlike PIC's limited I&R program, the Detroit Public Library established an I&R service in 1971 known as TIP (The Information Place) that involved the total library staff in the training and delivery of I&R services. Regarded as a priority service by the library administration, TIP became a model I&R service for public libraries by the mid-1970s.

In 1972, the first professional conference on information and referral services in public libraries was held at the University of Illinois. The issue that called forth heated debate was whether I&R is a professional library service or a casework service for professional social workers (Kronus & Crowe, 1972). A major federally funded project designed to study the effectiveness of library-based I&R services was the Urban Neighborhood Information Centers Project (NICs) that was conducted during a three-year period, from 1972 to 1975, in five major cities (Atlanta, Cleveland, Detroit, Houston, and Queens Borough, New York). While I&R programs developed differently in each of these urban sites, the project made a significant impact by demonstrating that the public library can effectively serve as a community information center and thereby expand its services far beyond the reference file. Since 1971, the American Library Association has recognized I&R as an important user-oriented service and has designated I&R as a vital goal for all public library services (Puryear, 1982).

A publication of selected library-based I&R programs and research studies edited by Kochen and Donohue (1076) reported empirical experiences and research findings of various library I&R programs. An overview of I&R in libraries, reported in a special issue of the *Drexel Quarterly* (Braverman, 1976), highlighted various perspectives on I&R programs that indicated support as well as resistance on the part of librarians engaging in I&R services. A book edited by Clara S. Jones (1978), former director of TIP at the Detroit Public Library, presented a prescriptive overview of I&R operations in public libraries. More recently, a nationwide survey of I&R programs in public libraries (Childers, 1984) reported on the differential development of I&R programs at the seven selected libraries. Based on the national survey findings and individual studies of I&R programs at the seven library sites, Childers urged librarians "to campaign for an altered set of service priorities for public libraries, a list in which I&R could perhaps displace in priority an existing service" (p. 60).

Another new setting that has assumed a growing importance for I&R programs since the early 1970s is the work place. Labor unions have traditionally sought to meet members' needs through the development of social services programs that are concerned with personal services related to housing, education, recreation, illness, and disability. Often wary of the formally organized social welfare agencies and suspicious of involvement with the formal social welfare community, organized labor's go-it-alone philosophy has led to the development of informal networks of I&R-type services that are operated by individual union leaders who function as advocates, using a family support approach. Under the auspices of the AFL-CIO Community Services Committee, I&R-type programs operate to assist union members with their problems both at and outside the work site (Perlow, 1979). Union counseling programs have also developed community-based programs in cooperation with other organizations, such as the United Way of America and the American Red Cross. Among various self-help community programs, Perlis reported "the firefighters" project to develop neighborhood information and referral centers that could operate on a 24-hour-a-day basis (Perlis, 1978).

Formal union programs have subsequently developed in which social workers train rank-and-file worker-volunteers to serve as information and referral agents at the work site. Various other union programs operate in combination with established social welfare agencies that provide I&R services. The United Way of America has initiated referral agent programs in which selected company employees are trained as I&R agents to serve their company personnel (1974, p. 199).

To meet child-care needs for working parents at a time when

government support for social services has been reduced, selected corporations have developed a variety of I&R programs, some of which operate onsite. A growing trend is to help parents locate satisfactory child-care resources through referral and collaboration with available and appropriate community I&R programs. The major motivation for the support of I&R day-care services by corporations has been to reduce employee absenteeism and promote productivity (Sallee & Berg, 1983). I&R developments in child care reflect the increased involvement of the private sector in social welfare services as public day-care services have been reduced and the volume of working mothers has increased. For growing numbers of profit-making organizations, I&R is a significant employee benefit that can operate in the interest of "good business."

New Service Groups

The human-rights movement that was initiated in the 1960s continued to generate new demands for services in the 1970s and identified new groups of users, for example, the handicapped, the unemployed, women, and children.

Although special programs for the disabled were included in the Social Security Act of 1935, minimal provision for access to services for the handicapped was available until the decade of the 1970s, which Bruck (1978) called "the decade of disability." The implementation of the Education for All Handicapped Children Act of 1975 required the "mainstreaming" of disabled children in public school programs and optimal utilization of resources in the integration of the handicapped into existing community service programs. The "Bill of Rights Act" of 1975 for the Developmentally Disabled (PL 94-103) clearly specified "maximum development under the least restrictive conditions." Formally organized advocacy programs, as well as informal self-help programs organized by and for the handicapped, have indicated the need for access to information on generic services as well as specialized resources. To promote the Independent Living Programs for the Disabled, the Information Center of Hampton Roads (Virginia) developed a specialized program of I&R services for the disabled within their generic program of services. On a national level, the

United States Clearinghouse on the Handicapped has been actively engaged in the compilation and dissemination of informational sources in the promotion of advocacy for the handicapped (Roth, 1981).

In 1976, Collins and Pancoast reported that their search for
I&R services within local communities led them to identify the
existence of natural helping systems. A major reason for the
organization of self-help groups has been the mutual need for all
participants to link up with available services. The proliferation of
self-help groups represents a diversified range of special interest
groups in need of information, referral, and advocacy to serve the
special interests of single parents, abused women, handicapped
persons, ethnic minorities and other interest groups. Self-help
groups have also developed on college campuses as hot-line and
drop-in services that are usually staffed by students who provide
information and peer counseling on a direct person-to-person
basis.

A Critical View—GAO Survey

A highly critical report of the planlessness and fragmentation of
I&R developments—*Information and Referral for People Needing
Human Services—A Complex System That Should Be Improved*—
was issued in 1978 by the U.S. General Accounting Office (GAO).
Based on a survey of 143 providers of I&R services,this report to
the Congress concluded that the erratic growth of I&R had
resulted in duplication, fragmentation, and inadequate services.
The GAO report ironically observed that those who provide information and referral services have themselves become part of
the maze on which they were supposed to offer guidance. A
major recommendation of the GAO report was the assignment of
a task force to develop "a national policy and plan to promote the
establishment of federal, comprehensive information and referral
centers" (U.S. General Accounting Office, 1978, p. 32).

THE 1980s—I&R NETWORKS

The need for improved coordination became increasingly urgent
as growing numbers of agencies continued to develop I&R pro-

grams without guidelines and well-planned coordination. In the wake of service cutbacks and major reductions in budgetary allocations, I&R agencies have attempted to minimize the negative effects of diminishing social services by maximizing access to existing services, thereby creating new partnerships and promoting interorganizational linkages. Another significant development has been the expanded role of the private sector in providing corporate support for I&R services for child care and in expanding employee benefits through I&R services in Employee Assistance Programs.

On a national level, the Administration on Aging (AoA) promoted the concept of networking through the establishment in 1974 of an Interdepartmental Task Force on Information and Referral that represented 15 federal departments and agencies. To promote networking, the AoA published an *I&R Guide*, which set forth baseline criteria for I&R service delivery, in 1977. For purposes of demonstrating the merits of interagency collaboration, coordination, and cooperation, statewide workshops on I&R networking were held in North Carolina (1979) and in Indiana (1980) under the sponsorship of the AoA Task Force.

New Partnerships and Coalitions

Due to various agency reorganizations and the loss of several agencies that were members of the task force, a new consortium was established by AoA in May 1983, with representatives from the public, voluntary, and private sectors. The aim of the AoA I&R Consortium, as defined in the minutes of the Consortium meeting on March 20, 1986, is the development of comprehensive community-based care systems with a coordinated base. The I&R Consortium is viewed as a vehicle to inform states and community agencies of the need for cooperative relationships necessary for the effective use of available resources and to promote the networking of I&R programs.

Additional Consortium members representing the voluntary sector include the United Way of America, the Alliance of Information and Referral Systems, and the American Association of Retired Persons (AARP). The inclusion of staff members from the United States Army, Community Services Division, reflects the

emerging interest of the armed forces in developing I&R programs within military installations as well as establishing linkages
with existing I&R programs. New consortium members from the
American Telephone and Telegraph Company (AT&T) represent
the growing involvement of the private corporate sector. Directories of toll-free telephone numbers published by AT&T, as well
as a new nationwide pricing plan for instate long-distance calling,
have expanded telephone communications, which, in turn, have
implications for I&R operations. In addition to designing new
products to meet the special communications needs of people
with disabilities, AT&T has also collaborated with other agencies
to set up a consumer hot-line to answer questions and facilitate
access to information and needed resources.

An Expanding Technology

A major factor in the expansion of I&R networks in the 1980s has
been the rapid advances in automation that have produced unprecedented capabilities in communications and intersystem
linkages. Centralization of data bases for systematic access,
storage, and retrieval has enhanced the selection and management of voluminous funds of data within interactive information
systems. The increasingly wider application of automation by
growing numbers of I&R agencies has promoted broader networks and interactive communication between I&R systems. The
potential for more effective and efficient delivery of human services through automated I&R operations is one of the major
challenges for I&R in its linkage role within the human service
field.

NATIONAL I&R MEMBERSHIP ORGANIZATIONS

The expansion of I&R programs in the 1970s and 1980s was in
great measure attributable to the continued promotion of I&R by
the United Way of America and the dynamic leadership of the
National Alliance of Information and Referral Systems, Inc.
(AIRS). It is noteworthy that the United Way initiated I&R pro-

grams within community health and welfare councils and federated funding organizations, and has continued to be a prime force in the promotion of I&R programs within its affiliates. The United Way formulated the first set of I&R standards in 1973 and designed one of the first services classification systems, which subsequently became a model service identification system for many I&R services thoughout the United States and Canada. Through its loan library, programmed manuals, training programs, and I&R round tables, the United Way has fostered educational programs for I&R directors within its affiliates and for referral agents within industrial settings. It is of special significance that the more recent development of the national Alliance of Information and Referral Systems, Inc., is a spinoff of the United Way.

Throughout the period of burgeoning social programs in the 1960s, there was little coordination between the diverse I&R programs that evolved. Roundtable sessions with directors of I&R programs were conducted under the sponsorship of the United Way at the annual National Conferences on Social Welfare. At the I&R roundtable discussion that was held at the 1970 National Conference on Social Welfare in Chicago, I&R directors expressed an interest in developing an independent membership organization. Again, at the national conference in Dallas in 1971, I&R directors reiterated the importance of establishing an independent national I&R organization to include the broad and diversified interests that were developing in I&R programs. At the Information and Referral Workshop held at the National Conference on Social Welfare in 1972, a resolution was passed authorizing the formation of a national professional organization to be known as the Alliance of Information and Referral Services (AIRS), available for membership to all individuals, groups, and organizations interested in or involved in I&R. Though supported initially by modest membership fees, AIRS was established in 1973 and expanded rapidly under the dynamic leadership of Corazon Estava Doyle, who served as volunteer executive director for seven consecutive years. (Significantly, AIRS was renamed the Alliance of Information and Referral Systems, Inc., in 1981.) After 1978 AIRS decided to conduct its own annual conferences, independent of the National Conferences on Social Welfare.

AIRS currently possesses a broad membership of more than 500 individuals, professional groups, and official I&R agencies and programs that operate within both the public, private, and voluntary sectors. In addition to formally organized I&R agencies, AIRS membership also includes hot-lines, self-help groups, and specialized informational services. AIRS has also produced and promoted a variety of publications in the field of I&R. Annual conference proceedings, published in 1974–1977, reflect the early organizational efforts of AIRS to establish a national presence. Since 1979, AIRS has published a newsletter for its members and produced a semi-annual professional *I&R Journal*. The joint effort in the compilation of the 1983 set of *National Standards for I&R* by the United Way of America and the Alliance of Information and Referral Systems, Inc., represents a significant collaborative achievement. AIRS' study of I&R Model Systems, which was supported by AoA funds and conducted by a research team at the Akron University Urban Center (1983), represents a major contribution to I&R research. The 1984 *Directory of I&R Services in the United States and Canada*, published by AIRS, is the latest inventory of I&R programs in North America. Along with its national expansion, AIRS has encouraged the development of state and regional chapters; as of 1984, 21 chapters were acknowledged as affiliates of AIRS.

VIEWING ACCESS SYSTEMS ABROAD:
CABs AND I&Rs

Growing interest in access systems abroad has stimulated interest in two major types of service systems: the British model of Citizens Advice Bureaux (CABs) and American-type I&R systems. As previously mentioned, the first study of the British CABs was reported by Kahn and his associates in a 1966 monograph, *Neighborhood Information Centers*, which exerted a profound influence on the development of I&R services in the United States. Although the CAB model was presented as an exemplary access system, it was apparent that replication of the CAB model in the United States was neither advisable nor possible. The only other cross-national report on access services prior to 1984 was the series of unpublished papers presented at the Conference of European Social Development Programs that was held in Washington, D.C., in October, 1979. This "Ten National Group Conference on Access to Social Services," which was co-sponsored by the American Public Welfare Association and the United Nations, recommended expansion of multinational communication and exchanges of information to promote access to human services (Tatara, 1979).

A more recent study of international access systems was reported by Levinson and Haynes (1984). Based on reports from nine developed and developing countries, the editors of this volume describe the enormous diversity and variations of access systems in countries in which access systems operate at various stages of development. Acknowledging that no composite or ideal model of an access system exists, the authors point to some common features and marked diversities between the British CAB model and the American I&R model.

Bearing in mind that the British CABs predated American I&R services by at least 20 years, and that these countries differ vastly in size, population, and sociopolitical conditions, there remain marked similarities as well as sharp differences between these two major access systems, as illustrated in Table 2-1. Although both the British CAB and the American I&R system combine elements of generic and specialized services, CABs are generally more committed to locally based generic service programs, while I&Rs have historically favored specialized services. Both access systems endorse advocacy measures in behalf of individuals or aggregates of users, though CABs tend to employ more aggressive advocacy measures.

In the United States there is no parallel to the hierarchical levels of organization that operate within the CAB system in the United Kingdom. Local CABs are governed by their own management committees and are responsible to regional CAB area committees, which in turn are accountable to the central office of the National Association of Citizens Advice Bureaux (NACAB) in London. American observers have been especially impressed with the extensive utilization of volunteers in CAB operations; they comprise 85 to 90 percent of all staff and receive mandatory training in information, advice-giving, and advocacy tactics in carrying out their responsibilities as direct service agents. The availability of volunteer lawyers (solicitors), as well as selected numbers of accountants and planners, contrasts sharply with the unavailability of these professionals as volunteers in I&R programs. Lacking the updated standardized resource files that are provided by NACAB and uniformly used by every CAB in Britain, American I&R programs operate under a myriad of different information systems, thereby rendering comparability of data almost impossible. As noted in Table 2-1, the role of CABs in national policy making and consultation to central government has distinguished CABs as official policy and planning bodies as well as service organizations. In contrast, I&Rs have neither been guided by national policy nor called upon to serve national purposes.

Both the British Citizens Advice Bureau and the American I&R models have influenced the organization of access systems in other developed and developing countries. Because of Canada's physical proximity to the United States, and because of funding supplied by the United Way of America to Canadian agencies, many Canadian I&R systems closely resemble the American I&R model. In those countries that have had an association with the British Commonwealth (e.g., Australia, India, Israel, and South Africa), access systems have tended to follow the CAB pattern of operation. Unique and innovative features of other access systems reported by Cyprus, Japan, and Poland reflect the particular sociocultural background of the countries and the idiosyncratic nature of their respective social welfare systems. In all of the reported access systems abroad, the role of the volunteer as a direct service agent is prominent. In addition to a focus on consumer-centered services, these cross-national reports emphasize the capabilities of organized access systems to contribute to social planning, policy formulation, and social reform (Levinson & Haynes, 1984).

SUMMARY

A genuine understanding of I&R has to take into consideration the recency and rapidity of its development. While origins of I&R-type programs have been traced to the social services exchanges of a century ago, I&R services are essentially a product of the 1960s that became institutionalized in I&R organizations during the 1970s and generated expanding I&R networks in the 1980s. To provide insight into the nature of I&R practice, the following two chapters analyze functional I&R service components (Chapter 3) and organizational structures in which I&R programs operate (Chapter 4).

II | I&R Practice: An Interactional Process

3 The Nature of I&R Services

"Defining the nature of I&R service is pertinent to how the general public is to be served. How I&R responds to inquiries defines the nature of its service."
—David M. Austin, *I&R: The New Glue for the Social Services*

A glance at a list of I&R agencies indicates that I&R organizations arc often identified by the specific and unique nature of the services provided. For example, rather than using the term *information and referral services,* some programs are identified as *information, referral, and follow-up services* (IRFSs), thus highlighting the follow-up aspects of the service. Those agencies that are identified as *information, referral, and retrieval services* (IRRs) call attention to the technical capability of the agency systematically to identify and retrieve information from resource files. The British term *Citizens Advice Bureaux* (CABs) focuses on the citizen as service user and magnifies the advice and advocacy functions of the CAB program. *Community Information Centers* (CICs) and *Neighborhood Information Centers* (NICs) generally represent locality-specific information and referral services that are often associated with I&R services in local public libraries. Specialized I&R services usually indicate I&R programs that are designed for specific target groups, such as the Women's Information, Referral and Education Service (WIRE), Referral and Information Service for the Elderly, or I&R for Runaway Youth. Irrespective of the diverse population groups for which I&R services are designed, there are significant commonalities as well as differences in the nature and delivery of all I&R services.

Because of the generalized application of the term *I&R* to many undefined service functions, it may be helpful to indicate what I&R is *not*. I&R is intended to be neither a clerical task nor a routine administrative function in a service agency. It operates as an information-assistance system rather than as an information-giving service, since both the consumer and provider are involved in an interactional process. I&R requires helping skills that go well beyond the mechanics of organizing and operating a resource file. Moreover, the published inventories of resources, no matter how well organized and compiled, do not *ipso facto* constitute an I&R service.

It should also be noted that I&R is *not* synonymous with information and retrieval, which is specifically designed for effective recall or extraction of information, rather than the provision of a consumer service. Nor is an I&R strictly a reference service that relies solely on published materials. Contrary to the views held by some agency personnel, I&R is not merely a screening mechanism; nor is it a routine intake procedure designed to determine whether the applicant can meet the eligibility requirements of the particular agency. Neither should I&R operate as a last resort for dead-end referrals when all prior efforts have been exhausted.

Some distinction should be made between I&R and the ombudsman function, since both respond to complaints from aggrieved consumers. Unlike the ombudsman, who usually serves as a mediator between the complaining consumer and the specific organization, the I&R agent acts primarily in behalf of the consumer and, if indicated, not only negotiates with the system but tries to change the system in order to accommodate the consumer's needs. Nevertheless, aspects of I&R may interface with the ombudsman function in the process of mediation.

In view of the diverse population groups served by I&R, there are significant differences in the nature and delivery of I&R services. The multiple settings, varied structures, and different agency auspices under which I&R programs operate contribute to the difficulty of classifying I&R services and categorizing I&R organizations. Interestingly, the diversity in I&R programs is also reflected in the varied terms that are applied to the I&R user, who is variously identified as the *client, patient, patron, consumer, recipient, beneficiary,* and *inquirer,* all terms that reflect differences in organizational auspices and variations in the nature of I&R services.

For purposes of analysis and comprehensiveness, the components of I&R services will be divided into two major categories—direct services to I&R clients or consumers and indirect services that deal with policy, planning, outreach, administration, and research related to I&R. But first, an examination of the various modes of entry to I&R services is necessary.

MODES OF ENTRY

The mode of entry to I&R services varies, depending on whether the initial request is made by telephone, by mail, or by walking in. In the United States, the telephone is the most prevalent mode of access to I&R services for inquirers. Telephone communications have been enhanced through toll-free 800 numbers, tie-lines, and such various technical capabilities as call-waiting, call-forwarding, and three-way calling, which link the client, the service provider, and the referral agent. While it is the goal of most I&R operations to provide 24-hour services, only 83 (14 percent) of 597 agencies reported in the 1984 AIRS Directory that they operate a round-the-clock service.

Many I&R agencies are increasingly utilizing answering machines and telephone recorders that request the inquirer to leave a message and a return number for call-back. According to the 1984 AIRS Directory, more than three-fifths, or 364, of the reported 597 I&R agencies had some type of after-hours arrangement. Some answering machines provide additional information and offer a choice of additional numbers to call in case of emergency. More than one-fifth (133) of the agencies reportedly used some type of recording apparatus or staff plan to document calls. About 10 percent (65) of the agencies handled after-hours calls by staff arrangement, and approximately 13 percent (78) of the agencies reported use of an answering service to respond to callers. Growing numbers of agencies also use call-forwarding mechanisms, which automatically transfer off-hours calls to another number for direct communication with a respondent. Through a call-forwarding arrangement, 15 percent (88) of reporting I&R agencies were able automatically to connect the caller to a responding agent.

Another mode of entry is the I&R walk-in service, which is the predominant pattern of access to information and advice reported by the Citizens Advice Bureaux in Great Britain. Walk-in services are usually conducted at convenient locations (such as town halls, public libraries, transit centers, or in store-front service centers) and are usually preferred by older citizens. When a face-to-face meeting is required for practical assistance in completing formal applications, or when a more detailed report or more accurate assessment is needed to arrive at a service plan, open-door services are exceedingly helpful. Of inestimable value is the walk-in service, which facilitates dropping in for support, reassurance, and an opportunity to talk out a concern, even if the I&R agency is not involved in an immediate follow-up plan. Since walk-in services require available staff who are prepared to respond directly to client inquiries, it is important to assess judiciously the demand and volume of services that could possibly be handled by the I&R service, else the demand may exceed the volume the I&R agency can provide.

For a variety of reasons, a limited but not insignificant number of requests are received by mail. One reason for mail inquiries may be the unavailability of a telephone or the inability to reach an I&R service by phone. For personal reasons, inquirers may be reluctant to ask for help or to discuss problems by telephone or walk-in due to embarrassment, stigma, or difficulties in articulation. The volume of written inquiries and the complexity of the requests determine the amount of staff time required to respond to mail requests. If the request is for a service that can best be handled by another agency, the client's permission must be obtained before sending a copy of the original letter to the appropriate agency. The rules and operational procedures that aim to safeguard confidentiality govern all aspects of I&R services.

I&R SERVICE CATEGORIES

In an effort to arrive at a logical classification of I&R services, various authorities have suggested different approaches. For example, Kahn (1969) makes a distinction between the "essential components" of information giving, advice, and referral, and the "optional components" in I&R programs, which include counseling, advocacy, outreach, consumer education, community planning, and various concrete services such as transportation and escort services. While acknowledging that the information-giving and referral aspects of an I&R program are the basic components, Long (1972) suggests a modular approach, whereby service modules can be added incrementally to an I&R program in accordance with the expectations of the community, the resources of the agency, and the capabilities of the staff to take on additional service responsibilities. Long observes that in some communities the basic information and referral service of the I&R center may be sufficient; in others, additional service functions may be provided, such as extensive follow-through, outreach, and escort services (Long, 1971). In analyzing library-based I&R programs, Childers (1984) distinguishes between "primary" and "secondary activities" based on particular kinds of activities. Included in "primary" activities are both simple and complex information giving and referral. Secondary activities involve advocacy, evaluation, and planning, but also include follow-up, which is usually considered a primary activity.

For purposes of this analysis, as mentioned earlier, I&R services are categorized according to *direct* and *indirect* service functions. These categories are not discrete but rather operate interactively. Rather than regarding I&R as a series of discrete program modules, I&R practice indicates that the elements or components of an I&R program are functionally interrelated and tend to be perceived as a continuum. The checkpoints on the continuum may range from assistance with information only, to advice, to brief or long-term counseling, and may even extend to diagnostic treatment at the far end of the continuum. The extent of information given may depend upon the nature of the specific inquiry and the level at which the information is appropriately shared with the inquirer. Given the complexity and multiplicity of human problems, what may initially appear as a request for simple information may in fact be a situation that requires handling beyond the capabilities of available I&R staff.

As illustrated in Table 3-1, direct I&R services are viewed as continua of functional components that range from "less intervention" to "more intervention" by the service provider. Information assistance, referral, and follow-up are viewed as the basic components. These tasks relate to the continuum of interpersonal relations that may range from information only (steering), to advice, to, conceivably, treatment. If language communication is a problem, translation services may be made available. To ensure client travel to a given destination, transportation and possibly personal escort services may be provided. In the event that the

TABLE 3-1 Extent of Provider Intervention in Direct I&R Services

Direct I&R Services	Extent of Provider Intervention		
	Less Intervention	————————————————→	More Intervention
Basic I&R components	Information assistance ——→	Referrals ——→	Follow-up
Support services	Translation ——→ services	Transportation —→	Escort services
Case advocacy	Registry of ——→ consumer complaints	Legal ———————→ assistance	Referral to professional legal services
Interpersonal relationships	Steering ———→	Counseling ——→	Treatment

client requires more intensive follow-through and support to redress a wrong or seek action on a complaint, case advocacy may be offered by the I&R agency that provides legal information or referral to professional legal services may be given for more complex legal matters.

Of equal importance are the indirect I&R services. Unlike case advocacy, which provides I&R services to individuals and their families, class advocacy is an action taken by an I&R agency in response to the needs and interests of aggregates of I&R users. Outreach and public relations, whereby I&R services are publicized and made known to potential users, are also of vital importance. And the importance of the planning and research components of I&R programs, which influence agency policy and determine operational guidelines for service delivery, is being increasingly recognized. The remainder of this chapter will elaborate further on the nature of client-focused direct services and the more organizationally focused indirect I&R services.

Direct I&R Services

Basic I&R Components

The basic functions of I&R involve assisting with needed information, providing referrals, and conducting follow-up.

Information Assistance The largest volume of requests for I&R services is in the area of "I" (information) rather than "R" (referral) on the continuum of I&R service delivery. The term *information assistance* is suggested in preference to the more frequently used *information giving* to connote an interactional process that focuses on the consumer as the information seeker in need of help or assistance from the service provider. General information assistance may be offered in response to simple and straightforward inquiries such as how to get a copy of a birth certificate or what veterans benefits are available to help finance graduate studies. Going beyond simple information inquiries, information may also be requested for more complex matters dealing with personal problem situations concerned with entitlements, benefits, or legal provision, as in the following inquiries:

"Can my mother-in-law be committed to a mental institution under nonvoluntary conditions?" "I have been fired twice within the past six months; how do I apply for unemployment compensation?" To respond to these inquiries, some background information about the inquirer is necessary in order to determine entitlements or potential eligibility.

Referrals Referral of the consumer to an appropriate service may require minimal or far more extensive intervention. The 1978 *AIRS Standards* indicate that little or no intervention is required for a simple referral, whereas a complex referral may call for participation and active intervention in linking the inquirer to the appropriate service. What is described as a simple referral is generally handled by the steering process described above (i.e., providing sufficient information for the inquirer to follow through independently). A complex referral may require more active intervention by the provider, such as making an appointment for the client with a staff member at another agency, writing a letter, or actually representing the client if necessary. What may initially appear to be a simple referral may, in fact, turn out to be a highly complex one. For example, a request for the address of a family planning agency may involve a simple referral to a public health clinic or to the office of a Planned Parenthood agency. However, when the same inquiry is presented with the additional information that, "I think I'm pregnant and my parents must not know," the referral process is no longer simple.

How a simple request can mount into a complex problem is illustrated further by the following example. An inquirer may ask for information on a local pharmacy at which to purchase medication at a discount rate. Further discussion may reveal that the caller is the mother of a seven-year-old child who has recently been diagnosed as epileptic. She notes that the child's father is currently unemployed and has incurred heavy debts to the extent that he is unable to meet the family's present living expenses and has no resources to meet the accumulated arrears. The care of two younger children, aged two and five, has ruled out the possibility of the mother's working. In addition to being overwhelmed with the child's diagnosis as epileptic, the mother states that she is particularly agitated by her husband's resentment that she did not tell him prior to their marriage that her maternal grandfather had epilepsy.

The complexity of this case may call for multiple referrals, repeated contacts with the inquirer, additional contacts with other members of the family, and a variety of referrals to relevant and appropriate agencies. Clearly, the complexities of the situation demand more than simple information assistance and referral.

Follow-Up Referral and follow-up are logically regarded as a dual process based on the assumption that a referral implies some measure of follow-up. However, in practice, follow-up on inquiries usually occurs only under special circumstances or as a requirement for a particular project or a special study. For example, the American Red Cross conducted a follow-up study of all cases referred by selected Social Security offices during 1971 to determine differential outcomes of I&R referrals. Universal follow-up was also reported in the WIS Project, undertaken by Interstudy in Wisconsin; every user of the service was given a choice to participate in the follow-up phase of the study (Long, 1976). Follow-up may be conducted on a sampling basis as was reported by the Information Center of Hampton Roads (Gilbert, 1975), which followed up on every tenth client contact for purposes of quality control and program evaluation. To monitor the I&R program for the elderly, follow-up was mandated by ICHR for every client over 60 years of age. Follow-up may also be conducted on a priority basis, the procedure followed by various I&R agencies in New York City that handled requests for fuel allowances during a severe cold spell in the winter.

In practice, I&R agencies conduct follow-up under any of the following conditions:

For all inquiries of apparent complexity that require further action beyond information only;

For situations in which more assistance is required to make the appropriate connection with the specific resource;

For referrals to services where there have been indications that clients are experiencing difficulties in completing the referral;

For situations requiring information on every person within a particular age group (e.g., teenagers or older citizens) in order to assess the nature and gravity of service needs or to assess outcomes of I&R services given;

For situations that warrant client advocacy and further provider intervention in order to negotiate for or represent the client;

For situations relevant to policy advocacy programs in order to document the incidence of a social concern or collective problem for aggregates of clients.

However the follow-up plan is carried out, it is important to bear in mind that sufficient staff time is required for systematic record-keeping and case management in monitoring the client's route through service systems of varying complexity.

The degree of worker involvement in follow-up is guided by a number of considerations. How much assistance is needed to help the client complete the referral? How much assistance will the client accept? What agency policies pertain to specific referrals in given problem situations? Answers to these questions will depend upon the worker's judgment of the client's capacity to follow through and a consideration of the individual client's circumstances, especially when danger to self and others may be involved. Fear and uncertainty may stymie the user's follow-through. Under some circumstances, it is advisable to telephone the agency while the client is still in the I&R office to arrange for the client to speak directly with the contact person at the referred agency, either to make an appointment or to offer explanation on the telephone. A client may appear to agree to a referral but, in fact, experience difficulty in accepting it or in following through with an initial contact with the referred service. Arrangements for escort and transportation may be necessary to provide the means whereby the client can assuredly reach the specific resource.

The main purpose of follow-up is to determine if the client service has been delivered and whether the outcome is satisfactory. At the time of the initial client contact, follow-up procedures need to be explained by the service provider, clearly indicating that it is carried out only with the user's consent (except under emergency or other unusual circumstances). To help guide staff in referral procedures, it is advisable that agency policies on current referral procedures be clearly spelled out in a set of instructions or a published manual. Why do some referrals fail or remain uncompleted? Possibly because the initial information provided to the user was insufficient, unclear, or inappropriate. If misinformation has been inadvertently given, efforts must be made to rectify the error promptly and enter the correct information into the agency resource files. Ideally, both the client and the referred agency are contacted in a follow-up plan. However, the more common practice is to contact the client; agency follow-up may entail issues of organizational competition or turf. A more subtle reason is that follow-up may imply an evaluative judgment of the performance of the referred agency by the referring I&R service.

In the final analysis, the degree of follow-up depends upon the gravity and complexity of the situation, the policy of the I&R organization, and the judgment of the I&R agent. It also depends upon the availability of resources, the limitations of staff time, and the costs involved. A critical issue in follow-up is confidentiality, since a formal referral usually requires identification of the caller by the referring agency.

Support Services

To carry out a responsible service, it is often necessary to provide support services, depending upon service needs. With the increased number of ethnic groups who have arrived in the United States since the 1970s, I&R agencies are finding that translation services are essential; growing numbers of I&R agencies are using bilingual volunteers and staff members. For example, the I&R center in Toronto maintains on call a staff capable of translating eight different languages. I&R agencies also produce bilingual directories to serve specific minority groups, such as the Service Directory for Chinatown in New York City. Translator services are also available in ethnic-specific I&R agencies, such as the Oriental I&R service in San Francisco and the Jewish I&R service in New York City. The New York library system publishes a bilingual resource directory in Spanish and English. In Montreal,

I&R services are conducted as a bilingual service in French and English; in Vancouver, British Columbia, multilingual I&R agencies serve the minority communities.

When travel to needed services is a problem for the client, I&R agencies may themselves provide transportaion or arrange for transportation with an outside agency. Relatively few I&R agencies operate agency-based transportation services despite the reported frequency of requests for transportation, particularly by older persons and residents in suburban and rural areas. Escort services may also be provided by I&R staff members to provide support, supply needed information, or negotiate with another service system in behalf of the client.

Case Advocacy

According to the United Way I&R course manual, "advocacy is the act of contacting an agency to which a client has been referred, and intervening on behalf of the client when the agency has been denied service for which the client is thought to be eligible" (1979, p.1). When the routes to available services are blocked, it may be necessary for the I&R agent to take on the role of case advocate. The assumption is that the person in need of services is unable to engage in self-advocacy. Under these conditions, case advocacy is conducted to remedy or ameliorate a particular problem or given situation for an individual or family. Such was the situation of an elderly man who lost his Medicaid card. When, upon his return to a clinic for a check-up for a broken arm that had recently been treated, he was refused clinic services, he called the I&R worker. After telephoning the assigned Medicaid worker in the department of social services but receiving a constant busy signal, the I&R agent contacted the clinic supervisor and requested that a temporary card be issued to the patient to permit him to keep his clinic appointment as scheduled. Subsequently the I&R agent, as the case advocate, followed through by informing the assigned social worker in the social services department about the circumstances and the action taken.

On an individual case basis, follow-up can help determine the extent to which case integration and accountability are actually achieved. Because follow-up activities reveal vital first-hand data on the quality and effectiveness of the services given or not given by the referred agency, documentation of the findings in follow-up is extremely important in assessing the individual agency's response and the adequacy of total community services.

When the client is unable to deal with the barriers to reaching services, or in situations where the client has been mistreated or inadequately dealt with, case advocacy may be the necessary course of action to make complaint or redress a grievance. In dealing with problems that involve organizational neglect or ineptitude in the delivery of client services, the case advocate may find it necessary to resort to higher levels of supervisory or administrative personnel. It may also be necessary to institute an appeal process or refer the client to a professional lawyer when further litigation is involved. To delineate professional roles that relate to the possible unauthorized practice of law, Kahn draws a distinction between "legal assistance," which can appropriately be supplied by an I&R agent, and "legal services," for which a client should be referred to a professional attorney (Kahn, 1966, pp. 98–107).

Interpersonal Relationships

The intensity of the interpersonal aspects of the I&R process tends to vary with the level of the working relationship required for an effective service to the inquirer by the provider. In the process of I&R counseling, the first step is usually to provide necessary assessment of the inquirer's presenting problem and to clarify the inquirer's circumstances. A further step may require suggesting a course of action, thereby exerting a greater degree of intervention by the provider. Based upon a delineation of the problem situation, the I&R provider may, upon a review of alternatives with the client, assign priorities to possible options and arrive at a plan for action. This process of advising and counseling may range from an immediate, short-term contact to a more extended service, possibly including treatment by designated staff who are appropriately assigned to provide this intensive level of service. More likely, a referral will be made by the I&R agent to an appropriate outside agency when in-depth counseling or therapy is indicated.

Operationally, the extent of counseling generally depends upon the nature of the inquiry and the service program of the particular I&R agency. The competence of the staff member to diagnose underlying problems, to clarify options, and to arrive at a course of action with the client is a key determinant in the interactional process of service delivery. In the previous example of the epileptic child, the I&R agent was forced to probe for underlying problems in the seemingly simple request for discount drugs. What did the I&R worker regard as the primary problem? The child's epilepsy? The husband's unemployment? The wife's overwhelming efforts to handle family pressures? The outcome of this case ultimately depended upon the I&R agent's delineation of the problem and the handling of referrals with the available and appropriate agencies. In order to meet some of the family's needs, referral agencies may involve not only drug discount suppliers, but also the child's local school, contact with the unemployment office, job-training programs for the father, referral to a family service agency or a mental health center, or other counseling services. Rather than engaging in multiple referrals, it is conceivable that the complex family problems may be most effectively handled by a single referral to a local chapter of the Epilepsy Foundation of America.

The referrals that are made to any of the agencies suggested above will significantly determine the ensuing course of action, depending upon the worker's advice at the point of inquiry and the capabilities of the family to follow through on the advice given. Even when the client appears quite able to manage without additional help, advice giving may be useful in the formalization of a plan, as was true in the case of a recently divorced woman concerned about the care of her 7-year-old twin sons. She requested a child-care helper for her sons after school hours. One of the twins tended to be asthmatic, particularly when the mother was away from home. Though she was currently working on a flexible part-time schedule near home, her earnings were insufficient. She needed more income to meet her expenses, and therefore wanted to consider the full-time job available to her at a further distance from her home. The mother asked the I&R worker for advice in fiscal management and child-care arrangements.

In responding to an I&R request, advice giving may deal with an immediate problem, such as the crisis situation of the inquirer whose house was destroyed in a fire, leaving the family homeless. Or the problem may be of a less immediate nature but nevertheless a pressing concern, as is the request of a former prisoner who, upon release, is finding difficulty in securing a job. The advice given to this inquirer will depend not only upon the available resources, but also on the choice of the referral agency, be it from a mental health agency, a hot-line, or a local employment agency.

At what point does advice giving interface with counseling and possibly treatment in the following situation? A troubled young man lives at home with his widowed mother, who has been depressed since his father died last year. He earns enough money to manage by himself and would like to live in his own apartment. But he feels guilty about moving out of his mother's home. When he tries to talk to his mother about a possible move, she becomes even more depressed and threatens suicide. Could the I&R agent help his mother? Adequate handling of this complicated family dilemma may entail extensive casework by trained social workers at another agency, to which the inquirer may appropriately be referred. The major task of the I&R worker in this case may be to apply referral skills to insure continuity and follow-through of services.

Opposing views have been expressed regarding the importance of casework in the I&R service delivery process. A report from the Information Center of Hampton Roads emphatically states that "casework is never done. . . . the Center should never duplicate direct services that are provided in the area but should function strictly in a communications and coordination role" (Gilbert, 1975). On the other hand, Mickelson defines I&R as a casework process, observing that there is "a gray area" between information seekers and problem solvers. His premise is that where the gravity of the inquirer's situation approaches a need for more complex problem solving and goes beyond information dispensing, a qualified professionally trained social worker should intervene (Mickelson, 1979).

Indirect Services

In addition to the direct services that involve an interpersonal encounter between the individual caller and the I&R service agent, I&R programs also include a broad array of indirect services, including policy or class advocacy, outreach, planning, and research. So vital are these indirect services to quality I&R practice that the future of all I&R services may ultimately depend upon the sound implementation and effective management of these indirect service components.

Policy Advocacy

Unlike case advocacy, which focuses on the individual client, policy or class advocacy is generally concerned with the experience of aggregates or collectives of consumers in I&R programs. The policy advocate may be involved in social action, legislative changes, or community education, depending on the area of concern.

To illustrate, an annual report of an I&R agency noted that more calls were received requesting transportation services for the elderly than were recorded for any other single category of consumer requests during that year. Upon staff review and approval from the executive board and other appropriate levels of agency administration, the I&R agency may consider any one of several alternative courses of action in arriving at a policy decision to meet transportation needs: A policy decision may be made that the I&R agency will operate its own minibus in a given area, provided that local fraternal and civic organizations will contribute to the purchase of a bus. Or the policy advocate may encourage concerned citizens to write to legislators requesting funds for a transportation plan that will be jointly supported by a grant from the state office on the aging and contributory funds from the local county. Another strategy may involve a series of radio announcements or TV shorts that will dramatize the plight of the elderly, who, because of lack of adequate transportation and as documented in I&R case records, do not have the means to reach available services. An even more effective tactic might be the formation of groups of elderly citizens known to the I&R agency who will campaign for transportation services by attending legislative sessions and conducting town-hall meetings for the general public. Another alternative might be recruiting volunteer groups to provide transportation under the general sponsorship of the I&R agency staff.

Based on systematically reported data, the I&R agency may consider any of the above options that could lead to changes in service provision. However, a caveat should be noted: Policy advocacy may alter the I&R agency's image, by converting it to a cause agency with a specific mission rather than serving as a universal, unbiased, open doorway to services.

Outreach and Publicity

An I&R service is usually activated by the client, with the I&R provider as responder or reactor. However, the I&R provider can assume the role of the initiator by reaching out to target groups to recruit potential clientele. Since the extent to which an I&R service is utilized depends upon the community's awareness of the service, a vigorous public relations program must be conducted to reach the uninformed and uninvolved but potentially interested consumer. When I&R services are unavailable or inaccessible because of the distance involved, outreach may involve the operation of mobile I&R services in remote rural areas or for a hard-to-reach elderly population in a suburaban or inner-city area. Systematic outreach may require a time-phased plan for canvassing potential consumers to inform them of the availability of I&R services. Emergency outreach programs may also be conducted by I&R agencies to alert the community to a common concern, a pending disaster, or such serious environmental problems as air pollution or lead poisoning. A public education program or possibly a survey may be conducted to inform the community about the high incidence of reported substance abuse or the problems of unemployed youth as reflected in I&R service requests. The American Red Cross has traditionally incorporated I&R expertise in training programs for disaster aid and emergency helping services. Various I&R outreach programs have been designed to help the "invisible elderly" to reach needed health and social services by canvassing local neighborhoods and engaging in publicity programs through public service announcements on radio and TV (Huttman, 1985).

One of the consequences of outreach efforts is the development of new groups of I&R consumers. For example, librarians discovered that library-based I&R programs have attracted a totally new group of inquirers, over and beyond the traditional book-borrowing patrons. On a cautious note, experience has indicated that when outreach programs generate new and heavy demands for services, consideration must be given to anticipated demand without exceeding the capacity and resources of the I&R agency.

Planning and Research

Data generated from the documentation of I&R services represent a valuable source of information on human needs and community resources. Systematically reported service statistics can reflect the adequacy, sufficiency, and quality of existing services. I&R is picturesquely described as "a window on the man in the street," since the data can provide valuable information on consumer characteristics as well as on the incidence and gravity of reported social problems (Kahn, 1966).

In order to utilize I&R data for planning purposes, it is necessary systematically to compile selected data on resources and service statistics that can be shared with inhouse staff and with other organizations for purposes of policy formulation and decision making. Authorities differ about the extent to which I&R operators should be involved in the planning process. Long refers to the "planning support function" of I&R, noting that the information and referral agency need not, and in fact should not, become directly involved in the planning or decision-making processes within the community (Long et al., 1974). A contrary view is expressed by Zimmerman, who argues that I&R operators should be directly involved in planning and that planners should participate in all phases of I&R data selection, compilation, and dissemination. Based on an extensive study of the I&R program in the Minneapolis Department of Social Services, Zimmerman concludes that planning data should be established as an inherent component of I&R operations, rather than as an end-product or a peripheral activity (Zimmerman, 1977).

Optimal utilization of I&R data for planning purposes requires documented data that are valid and applicable to sufficiently large numbers of clientele to support the reliability of the reported data. To overcome possible resistance to documentation, involvement of I&R staff in the early phases of data selection and explanation of why and how the data will be used are necessary. To arrive at clear instructions for documentation, a testing period can be helpful to revise and modify data forms as indicated. In considering the extent to which I&R data may be used for social planning purposes, Long observes rather soberly that social planning is essentially a political process in which decisions are often arrived at to accommodate political pressures, irrespective of the nature of the data findings (Long, 1971, pp. 36–37). Nevertheless, given the need for empirical data and the dearth of reported service statistics, I&R programs can provide essential data bases for rational decision making and budgetary allocations in social planning. However, the validity of the data reported will depend upon whether the I&R services meet acceptable standards and criteria.

STANDARDS AND CRITERIA

While there are neither official mandatory standards for the operation of I&R services nor regulatory measures to enforce them, various sets of standards have been developed with varying levels of specificity. An early set of I&R standards was incorporated in the 1967 Brandeis survey (Bloksberg & Caso, 1967), which suggested the following minimal criteria for an I&R service:

- The information and referral service must be an organized service;
- At least one part-time staff person must be attached to the service;
- The staff must be formally designated to conduct the service;
- The agency must maintain an accurate resource file of agencies and services available in the community;
- The I&R agency or subunit must provide information and referral service as its primary task.

These standards have served as a helpful precedent and guided subsequent efforts in formulating acceptable I&R standards.

The first set of standards that specified criteria for quality I&R practice was published by the United Way of America in 1973. Basic requirements for I&R operations were developed by the Administration on Aging in 1974 that included short-range and long-range goals and emphasized the need for training, for both paid and volunteer staff. In order to evaluate the volume and quality of I&R service providers in the United States, the General Accounting Office conducted a survey of selected I&R programs that were evaluated according to a minimal set of selected standards. The findings of the survey indicated that a large number of I&R providers failed to meet the defined I&R standards because of inadequate resource files (53.1%), inadequate follow-up (45.5%), insufficient publicity (41.3%), and lack of outreach (73.4%). These reported results reflect the high degree of noncompliance and the absence of a recognized regulatory body to enforce an apparently minimal set of standards for I&R practice (USGAO, 1978).

The standards published by the Alliance of Information and Referral Systems, Inc. (AIRS) in 1975 were essentially an elaboration of the 1973 United Way standards but also included a requirement for client advocacy. In a second edition of the AIRS standards in 1978, policy advocacy and planning were added to the delineated standards. While outreach was recognized as an essential component of I&R in the preface of the AIRS 1978 standards, outreach was not included until the 1983 publication of the national I&R Standards that were jointly compiled by AIRS and the United Way of America. (A summary of the 1983 standards is included in Appendix C.)

Should the quality of I&R services fall below an acceptable level, it is difficult to challenge the quality of services in the absence of a national regulatory and accrediting body. Individual I&R agencies have developed their own self-evaluation instruments to test agency performance. The United Way developed an I&R Service Self-Evaluation Checklist based on its first set of I&R standards (1978). An elaborate research-oriented, self-evaluation kit was designed in 1982 for use by Community Information Centers in Toronto and published in nine separate sections by the Ministry of Citizenship and Culture in Ontario. Most currently, the National Alliance of I&R Systems (AIRS) has published a self-evaluation manual for I&R agencies (1987) that will establish a basis for accreditation. The expectation is that accreditation will promote and maintain high-quality professional practice based on compliance with the national standards for I&R formulated jointly by the United Way and AIRS in 1984 (Jacobson, 1986).

Essential Attributes of an I&R Service

In the ongoing process of formulating acceptable standards and criteria for I&R practice, there appears to be a growing consensus on the various qualities that are considered essential for acceptable I&R practice. The following is a suggested checklist of essential attributes for I&R services.

Availability: Is the I&R service universally available, unbiased, and nonpartisan? Are extended waiting periods avoided? Are services offered as purported?

Accessibility: Can the service be conveniently reached? Are phone lines open for calls? Is physical entry uncomplicated? Can the inquirer make direct contact with I&R staff or independently use resource files?

Appropriateness: Does the I&R program meet the needs and preferences of the general population or specific target group it aims to serve? Is the atmosphere congenial and friendly? Is the office neatly furnished?

Adequacy: Is the I&R service designed to meet the range and magnitude of needs of the intended clientele? Are there adequately trained staff and sufficient staff supports to meet service requirements?

Accountability: Is the I&R service responsible to the community, to the agency's board of directors, to the individual consumer? Do internal procedures assure this accountability?

Assured Confidentiality: What safeguards for privacy and confidentiality are provided by the I&R agency? Are security measures clearly defined and properly enforced?

Affordability: Can consumers reach services without undue expense? Can providers finance the basic I&R service with the current and projected funding available? Can I&R programs continue to operate if or when special project funds are terminated?

Acceptability: Are people in all socioeconomic groups receptive to I&R as a public service or social utility? Does the consumer feel welcome and comfortable in the particular agency setting in which I&R operates?

Adaptability: Is the I&R system sensitive to current social needs and responsive to organizational changes, policy shifts, new legislative mandates, and administrative realignments?

Assessability: What measures are taken at what intervals of time to evaluate the I&R agency program? Is the evaluation conducted by outside sources or as a self-study? Are long-term gains as well as short-term benefits taken into account? What are the social as well as the fiscal costs in assessing the effectiveness and efficiency of I&R services?

The above qualities are not weighted according to importance, nor are these items discrete. Rather, it is these attributes combined that represent the essentials of quality practice.

SUMMARY

I&R services include both direct services to clientele and indirect services that are essential to organizational maintenance and programming. As a direct service, I&R tends to function as a reactive service in its response to the demands of consumers. However, given the capability of I&R to provide data for research, policy formulation, and planning, I&R has the capacity to assume a proactive stance in highlighting service needs, advocating change, and introducing innovation. The extent to which I&R can effectively deliver quality services and facilitate improved access to services strongly depends upon the structural and managerial aspects of I&R organizations, as described in Chapter 4.

4 The Organizational Context

"It is important to distinguish between the activities carried out under the name of information and referral and the setting or manner in which such activities are discharged. The setting and functions are often confused."
—Nicholas Long, *Information and Referral Services: A Short History and Some Recommendations*

The diversity and complexity of I&R organizational structures defy a neat categorization of I&R agencies. No two I&R organizations are exactly comparable, nor are any two I&R service programs replicable. The size of I&R organizations does not necessarily reflect the size of the population served, nor does the volume indicate the severity of problems that exist in any one community. I&R services may range from a one-person, one-phone operation to an extensive statewide computerized program that handles hundreds of calls a day. Even seemingly similar I&R services offered to comparable clientele vary drastically in range, scope, and quality of services.

Because of these variations and the many factors that determine the range and quality of I&R programs, including funding resources, staff patterns, and community sanction and support, it is difficult to arrive at an ideal or optimal model of I&R operations. Nevertheless, an analysis of I&R organizations requires distinguishing between agencies that aim to serve universal needs of all people and agencies that focus on the special needs of individuals and groups. Based on the underpinning concept of I&R as a set of systems, a typology of organized I&R systems is presented that includes service systems, agency systems, and network systems. Before discussing the various kinds of organizational I&R patterns and agency structures, attention is directed to the distribution of I&R agencies within the United States.

REGIONAL DISTRIBUTION OF I&R AGENCIES

As shown in Figure 4-1, over half of I&R agencies (52.1%) are located in eastern states (within the regions labeled northeast and southeast), comprising almost half the states in the United States. In the remaining 26 states, the volume of I&R agencies is equally distributed between the 13 states in the north central and the south central regions (27.64%) and the 13 states in the northwest and southwest regions (20.28%), with some variations in total percentages of agencies included in each of these regions. It is interesting to note that the I&R agencies located in the 30 states in the northern parts of the country (northeast, north central, and northwest) comprise almost two-thirds (64.66%) of all I&R agencies reported, whereas in the southern half of the country (southeast, south central, and southwest), 21 states reported somewhat more than one-third (35.36%) of all I&R agencies. (See Appendix B for a list of states comprising each region.)

All states reported at least one I&R operation (Alaska), and the

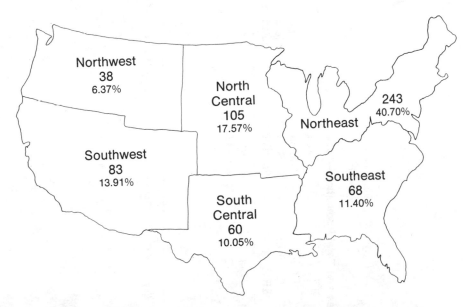

FIGURE 4-1 Regional distribution of I&R agencies by totals and percentages reported in 1984 (Data reported by individual state in Appendix B.)

Source: Alliance of Information and Referral Systems, Inc. (1984). *Directory of information and referral services in the United States and Canada.* Indianapolis: Author.

total number ranged as high as 52 I&R agencies (California). The six states that reported the largest number of I&R agencies (California, Illinois, New York, Ohio, Pennsylvania, and Texas) are located in four of the six regions of the country (northeast, southwest, south central, and north central), thus indicating a fairly wide distribution of the total volume of I&R organizations throughout the United States. In the southeast region, Florida reported the largest number of I&R agencies (17), while Oregon and Washington have the largest number of I&R agencies (12 each) reported in the northwest region. In each of the six highest-volume states (see Table 4-1), the number of I&R organizations bears a close relation to the total population of the state—since the six states with the largest number of I&R agencies are also the six highest-ranking states in population. California and New York ranked highest in both total population and total I&R agencies. While Ohio ranks third in the number of I&R agencies, it is sixth

TABLE 4-1 Highest Ranking States Reported by Total I&R Agencies and Total Population—1984

State	Region	Total I&R Agencies*	Rank Order of I&R Agencies	Total Population of States** (in millions)	Rank Order of Population
California	Southwest	52	1	27.7	1
New York	Northeast	45	2	17.5	2
Ohio	Northeast	43	3	10.8	6
Pennsylvania	Northeast	32	4.5	11.9	4
Texas	South Central	32	4.5	14.2	3
Illinois	North Central	31	5	11.4	5

* Source: Alliance of Information and Referral Systems, Inc. (1984). *Directory of information and referral sources in the United States and Canada.* Indianapolis: Author.
**U.S. Census, 1984 Supplement.

in total population. Pennsylvania and Texas tie for fourth in rank order of I&R agencies, while Illinois ranks fifth in both total I&R agencies and total population. Except for Pennsylvania, which ranked eighth in the 1978 inventory, the other five states were also among the highest-ranking states listed in the 1978 AIRS directory, indicating that I&R has continued to expand in these already high-ranking states.

GENERAL AND SPECIALIZED I&R PROGRAMS

As noted in Chapter 2, organized I&R services developed concurrently within two major categories: generic and specialized services. Characteristic of American social welfare, the early development of I&R favored categorical I&R services in the 1960s, particularly in the fields of health, mental health, and the elderly (Bloksberg & Caso, 1967). By the mid-1970s the shift toward generic services became more apparent. As many as two-thirds of the 616 agencies listed in the 1978 AIRS directory reported that their I&R services were generic; whereas slightly less than one-quarter of the agencies (24.9%) indicated that they provide only specialized I&R services. Similarily, a larger proportion of generic services compared to specialized services was reported in the AIRS 1984 directory. Almost two-thirds (378) of all the I&R agencies listed in the AIRS directory reported generic programs; the remaining 219 agencies, or approximately one-third, described their programs as specialized. Although very few agencies reported that they offer a combined generic/specialized program, I&R history indicates that generic and specialized services have developed concurrently, depending on funding patterns and the level of interorganizational cooperation. The budgetary restrictions of the 1980s highlighted the need to coordinate specialized and generic services in the interest of cost efficiency and more coordinated service delivery.

According to the United Way of America, a generic or comprehensive I&R is "an organization or function of an organization which provides information and referral to the general public regardless of need" (United Way, 1979, p. 1). In principle, all I&R services are generic, since I&R facilitates access to all human services and is presumably available to all citizens. Ideally, all I&R services provide a universal doorway to services, irrespective of whether the I&R program responds to requests for general or specialized information.

The model of the Citizens Advice Bureau comes closest perhaps to resembling the ideal type of generic, autonomous, community-based organization that is available to all citizens. In the United States, the social welfare legislation that most effectively advanced the generic I&R services model was incorporated into the Title XX amendments of the Social Security Act of 1974, which designated I&R as a universal service for all inquirers regardless of income. The absence of a means test for I&R services and the availability of I&R for all citizens, not only for clients of public welfare, signified an important application of universalism in I&R.

Beginning with the late 1950s, and continuing throughout the 1960s, consumer demands and expectations, coupled with the support of special interest groups, highlighted the need for specialized services by specific target groups. Among the specialized services that received funding were I&R programs for the elderly, the chronically ill, the handicapped, and the mentally ill. Since the 1970s, there has been an expansion of I&R programs for children and youth, and more recently, for the disabled and women. As shown in Table 4-2, an overview of specialized I&R programs suggests three major categories of I&R programs. The first category is classified according to the target population involved; that is, by age (elderly, children, and youth) and by gender. I&R programs that are involved with particular health and social problems constitute the second category. A third category of I&R services is defined on the basis of organizational association or affiliation and includes ethnic/religious groups, membership organizations (e.g., labor unions), and status groups (e.g., veterans).

In viewing the list of specialized I&R programs, it should be noted that specialized I&R services do not necessarily represent discrete or single-service categories. In fact, two or more categorical services may be included in an I&R program that combines, for example, the aging and the handicapped, children and youth, alcohol and drug abusers, women and children. Another observation is that specialized I&R programs may be designed to

TABLE 4-2 Categories of Specialized I&R Programs

By Age and Gender

Elderly
Children/youth
Women/men

By Problem Area

Health disorders
Mental illness
Drug and alcohol abuse
Handicapping conditions

By Membership/Affiliation

Ethnic/religious groups
Membership groups; e.g., labor unions & self-help groups
Status groups; e.g., veterans, students

serve even more highly specialized subcategories of I&R users, such as services for the frail elderly, run-away youth, divorced fathers, or families of prisoners. The ensuing discussion will elaborate further on these specialized I&R programs.

By Age and Gender

The fact that almost 80% of the 616 I&R agencies reported in the 1978 AIRS directory dealt specifically with the aging population reflects the predominance of I&R services for older persons. Several factors may account for this strong interest in I&R for older adults; namely, the acknowledgment of the multifaceted needs of a rapidly growing older population, the impact of "senior-power" advocacy programs, and the initiatives of the Administration on Aging, the only federal agency with a clearly defined mandate for I&R services. As for the wide range of needs, it is reported that older people have the lowest incomes and incur the highest medical expenses compared to the total population. The elderly spend the highest proportion of their incomes for the basic needs of food, shelter, and utilities, and they live in the poorest housing. Personal problems are compounded for the rapidly expanding older population, many of whom are dependent upon fixed incomes, and particularly for the elderly who have some degree of physical or mental impairment (Huttman, 1985). It is therefore not surprising that the strongest thrust for I&R services has been targeted to the elderly population.

Specialized services for children with problems have a long and venerable history in American social welfare services. However, limited provision has been made for universal services that can promote the welfare of *all* children. Information and referral services for children have emerged primarily for children involved in foster care, adoption, or child abuse. New York City was in the vanguard in the introduction of an information system to monitor the child foster-care program. The voluntary agencies in New York City, which care for about 80% of the city's foster-care population, began to consider an automated information-processing system, through a purchase of services arrangement, as early as 1969. With the public sector's cooperation and support, an independent Child Welfare Information System (CWIS) has been in operation since 1975 (Greenspan, 1979).

Interest in I&R services for children and youth increased in the 1970s when the movement for child advocacy gained momentum and the developmental and social needs of all children gained prominence. While the publicity on the "Year of the Child" in 1979 resulted in more rhetoric than actual improvement in social provisions for children, it did dramatize the plight of children who are deprived of access to needed health care and social services. A paucity of I&R agencies reported specific services to children in the 1978 AIRS directory; however, specialized I&R programs for children appear more frequently in the 1984 directory.

A variety of I&R-related programs designed to promote the welfare of children has developed in both the public and private sectors. For example, the Help for Children program was created by the Massachusetts legislature in 1972 with a commitment to deliver and monitor I&R services at local, area, regional, and state levels. The thrust of the Help for Children program was to provide information, referral, follow-up, and advocacy to children and their families, and to supply data on children's services based on the reports of staff assigned to local councils within the state network.

Another type of child-centered I&R agency is the Specialized

Child Health Center in Ottumawa, Iowa, which operates an I&R crisis intervention program. The center uses a toll-free phone number with incoming watts lines and maintains extensions to major resources on a 24-hour service through an agency tie-in system. A corporation-funded day-care system, utilizing resource and referral (R&R), has recently been developed in California to provide information and referral services to parents in search of day care for their children (Siegel, 1984). The trend toward corporate-sponsored information and referral programs for child day care is viewed by Sallee and Berg (1983) as an important trend and suggests a strong potential for the significant expansion of day-care services through corporate-funded programs.

While no specific I&R program exclusively for women is listed in the 1978 AIRS directory, specialized I&R services for women, in the form of hot-lines, mobile units, and even free-standing agencies, were established by the 1980s. Special lists of resources for women were added to published directories, and special units or departments within existing agencies were designated as I&R services for women, as noted in the Directory of the Community Resource Information Bureau (CRIB) for Services for Women published by the California State Department of Social Services in 1978. Information and referral services for women tend to respond to the needs of widows, divorcees, displaced homemakers, and abused women who are interested in legal information on separation, alimony, and divorce. Other areas of women-oriented I&R inquiries include child care, job training, employment, and opportunities for socialization. To deal with some of the socio-economic problems in child-rearing practices, particularly as experienced by the single, female head of a household, help is often sought through mutual aid or self-help groups in which self-selected leaders tend to assume responsibility for making connections with existing information and referral services.

Women's Information, Referral and Education Service (WIRE) was established in 1978 in the Boston area as a Junior League project. Trained volunteers as well as paid personnel operated a mobile Women's Van and provided 24-hour telephone service for emergency and general information to women until 1984, when the Women's Van program expanded to serve not only women but all other inquirers, reflecting the developmental trend of incorporating specialized services into broader generic I&R programs.

A growing number of men's groups, which reflect the capabilities of I&R services to assist men in their various roles as divorced persons, single fathers, widowers, and Big Brothers to young children, have also evolved since the early 1980s.

By Problem Areas

Despite the steady proliferation of health and social services since the mid-1930s, reaching health care services has remained a persistent problem. Notwithstanding the impressive technological advances of American medicine, systematic access to health services is often not available to those in need of care. In addition to the many barriers to services cited in Chapter 1, the health consumer remains uniquely disadvantaged, since reaching care is often not determined by free choice in an open and competitive marketplace. And because illness is often episodic, potentially serious, and always unplanned, the lack of access to appropriate health care has life-threatening implications. Therefore, early and effective information and referral services can provide vital preventive measures, as demonstrated in the operation of health information services, hot-lines, and the rapid expansion of the telephone-cassette information system of Tel-Med since 1973.

In the absence of the sort of national insurance plan that exists in most industrial nations in the world, entry to health care services in the United States is complex, capricious, and often very expensive. As the costs of health and medical care have soared, the barriers to care have continued to mount because of fragmentation, specialization, and the maldistribution of health facilities and health care providers. As noted in Chapter 2, the early history of I&R is bound up with concern for access to health services, particularly for the chronically ill and the elderly. The rising incidence of chronic illness in the aging population has highlighted the need for access to community-based services. As reported in the 1967 Brandeis survey of I&R services, a preponderance of specialized I&R services was reported in the fields of alcoholism and drug abuse, two health areas in which I&R programs have continued to expand. The I&R programs that were established in the early 1960s focused heavily on emergency services and hot-line services that dealt particularly with suicide prevention and crisis intervention (Bolch, Long, & Dewey, 1972). As the need for specialized crisis intervention facilities has become more widely recognized in suicide prevention programs (Roberts & Grau, 1970), a wide variety of I&R programs has been established in different organizational settings—as hospital-based emergency services, as telephone hotlines, and as neighborhood walk-in services. The AID Service of Edmonton in Alberta, Canada, is an interesting example of a suicide hot-line service that operates concurrently with the city's central I&R automated system. AID also provides a Family Bereavement Program for the relatives of families of suicide victims. Similar support groups are operated for both Survivors of Suicide (SOS) and Survivors of Homicide (SOH) at the Emergency Telephone Service/Suicide Prevention Center in Detroit as part of a community mental health program.

An example of a national computer-operated crisis service that is operated by trained volunteers is the VD (venereal disease) hot-line in Palo Alto, California. The VD hot-line maintains an updated resource file of over 5,000 facilities, 3,000 interactive crisis lines, and 1,000 private physicians who are available for referral. The capabilities of the automated system and the high level of volunteer training account for the reported effectiveness of this nationwide service (Mandel, 1983).

Specialized I&R services tend to focus on specific health disorders, such as the Can-Dial Service for persons inquiring about cancer and cancer care. Hot-line services have also been established to respond to a host of health problems related to kidney dialysis, epilepsy, stroke, diabetes, and various postoperative conditions, such as the Woman-to-Woman Hotline for postmastectomy patients at the Social Services Center of the Adelphi University School of Social Work. In the early 1960s, the Easter Seal Society not only established its own national I&R program to serve the handicapped, but also extended its I&R program to provide general I&R services to all inquirers through its local chapters.

Although Title II of the Mental Retardation Facilities and Community Mental Health Centers Act of 1963 stipulated that persons receiving services within a designated catchment area should have access to all health and social services, the movement toward deinstitutionalization of hospitalized mental patients, which gained momentum during the seventies, dramatized the unavailability and inaccessibility of adequate community services.

According to Bruck (1978), the 1970s represented "the decade of the disabled," with the passage of the "Handicapped Bill of Rights" in 1975 (PL 94-103); during this period, I&R services gained a new recognition as a linking mechanism to existing services. On the community level, a wide and complex array of information and referral activities have evolved under the sponsorship of parent information centers, mayors' offices, and state councils for the handicapped, and state-operated protection and advocacy offices for the developmentally disabled. Local chapters of national voluntary health organizations, as well as grassroots organizations for the handicapped, have sought to connect with available local I&R services. Advocacy programs designed to promote mainstreaming and independent living for the disabled have pointed to the need for I&R data to promote coordination and interagency linkages.

In response to the increased demand for systematized information on health resources, extensive volumes of published directories and advocacy materials have become available, such as the *Directory of National Level Information Sources on Handicapped Conditions and Related Services (1980)*, which lists over 100 voluntary organizations and federal agencies that relate to the handicapped. While many directories, handbooks, and manuals continue to be produced, the central I&R task is to translate published lists of resources into responsible and reliable human services, particularly at the point of inquiry, which is usually at the level of the local consumer.

By Membership/Status

Specialized I&R services have been organized by sectarian organizations and members of particular ethnic groups. Various I&R-type services are provided for newly arrived ethnic groups in need of information and referral for jobs and employment, schooling, vocational training, housing, and acculturation. A re-

cent development is the Foreign-Born Information and Referral
Network located in the Family Life Center in Columbia, Maryland, which also offers information on citizenship, consumer matters, child care, and medical facilities. An ethnic-specific service
is the I&R Service for Chinese Newcomers, designed to accommodate the Chinese immigrant. Since 1977, information and
referral services have been established in the New York City office of the Jewish Federation, which extends its services to all
callers, most of whom are Jewish. Jewish clientele are concerned
not only with the problems of the elder residents in the inner city,
but also with the plight of victims of the Holocaust and the more
recently arrived Russian Jewish refugees. While the sectarian social agencies, including Catholic Charities and Lutheran Social
Services, tend to attract and appeal to clientele who are members
of these respective faiths, I&R generally operates as a non-
denominational service and is available to all callers at the initial
point of inquiry.

The work place has historically provided union counselors to
assist union members with their personal problems and concerns.
Expanding interest in employee problems by corporate management, particularly in relation to alcoholism and drug problems,
has led to organized efforts to help employees function more adequately on the job, thereby maximizing production and minimiz-
ing staff turnover. Since the early 1970s, management-based I&R
services have developed employment-assistance programs
(EAPs) to provide employees on-site information or referral to
other counseling services. The United Way of America has
developed another type of I&R program related to the work site,
known as the Referral Agent Program (RAP). United Way staff
train selected personnel as RAP agents, who then conduct information and referral services for their company employees.

As discussed in Chapter 2, Veterans Information Centers
(VICs) were an important I&R prototype following World War II,
providing veterans with access to services to help in the adjust-
ment to civilian life. As growing numbers of veterans of World
War II have joined the ranks of the elderly in the past 25 years,
their need for increased utilization of available community resources has become a priority concern for the Veterans Administration. Community information and referral services are desig-

nated under the Veterans Health Expansion Act (P.L. 93-82), which permits eligible veterans to be treated in an ambulatory setting to obviate the need for hospitalization without regard for service connection. The result has been a steady expansion of outpatient and satellite clinics that serve increased numbers of veterans. Because a far larger volume of potential users among aging veterans is anticipated, I&R is viewed as a practical and potentially helpful link in connecting VA beneficiaries with other existing health and social service programs, as well as VA-based services.

Interest in the development of I&R services in the VA was spurred by the 1974 working agreement on "I&R Services for Older People Among Federal Departments and Agencies" initiated by the Administration on Aging. In accordance with this agreement, I&R representatives were appointed at each VA field station to provide a full range of VA services in collaboration with regional, state, and local Area Agencies on Aging (AAAs). A 1980 report by Program Analyst D. J. Schoeps of the Veterans Administration stated that within VA-oriented I&R programs I&R providers consisted primarily of professional social workers (106) and benefit counselors (27). In collaboration with the AoA, the Veterans Administration co-sponsored a series of I&R training programs in 1978–1980, attended by social workers from the Department of Medicine and Surgery and benefit counselors from the Department of Veterans Benefits. The I&R training programs indicated the need for closer cooperation between the social workers and the benefit counselors within the VA and recommended a stronger collaboration between the VA and other human service organizations.

As categorical and generic I&R services have continued to develop concurrently, two trends have become evident. Although I&R services often begin as specialized services for target populations, such as the handicapped, abused women, or the elderly, requests for general information inevitably impel the I&R agency to seek this information from other agencies or to make direct referrals to other appropriate sources. The tendency for specialized I&R services such as age-segregated services or problem-specific inquiries to evolve into more generic, age-integrated services was supported by an early research study conducted by Battle Associates (1977).

A second and contrary trend indicates that as general I&R services expand to include larger groups of users, the need for specialized information becomes more apparent. If the specialized service is not available within the agency's own range of services, appropriate referrals must be made. Interestingly, the trend toward a generic-based access system in the Citizens Advice Bureaux of Great Britian has shifted toward increased specialization within the CAB generic programs. Since 1980, paid specialists in marital and family counseling, welfare benefits, and housing and consumer affairs have been added to CAB's predominantly volunteer-operated staff (National Association of Citizens Advice Bureaux (NACAB) Annual Report 1980-1981, 1983-1984). A major organizational challenge in all I&R programs is how to incorporate and integrate specialized and generic I&R services in ways that can meet the general needs of total populations as well as the specific needs of target groups.

A TYPOLOGY OF I&R SYSTEMS

Because I&R represents mixed types and unique hybrids of organizational structures, it is difficult to delineate discrete types of I&R organizations. In an effort to arrive at a categorization of the widely diversified organizational structures of I&R, the following typology of systems and subsystems is proposed: information service systems that focus on the *functional* aspects of I&R, agency systems that embody the *structural* aspects, and networks that represent the *operational* aspects. As illustrated in Figure 4-2, the first category represents informational I&R service systems. The second category includes structural variations of organizational I&R systems that are designated as free-standing I&R agency systems, and I&R subsystems that are located within host agencies (interagency systems) and parent agencies (intra-agency systems). A third major category includes networks of multiple I&R agencies that operate as centralized or decentralized networks. A discussion of each of these categories will indicate the extensive range and wide diversity of I&R organizations.

FIGURE 4-2 A typology of I&R organizational systems

TYPES OF I&R SYSTEMS	DESCRIPTION OF TYPES OF I&R SYSTEMS	CONFIGURATION OF I&R SYSTEMS
INFORMATIONAL I&R SYSTEMS	An *Informational I&R System* provides information-assistance to all inquirers (phone, walk in or by correspondence).	
I and R AGENCY-BASED SUB-SYSTEMS	A *Free-Standing I&R Agency System* operates independently and autonomously. I&R is the single, generic service provided to clientele.	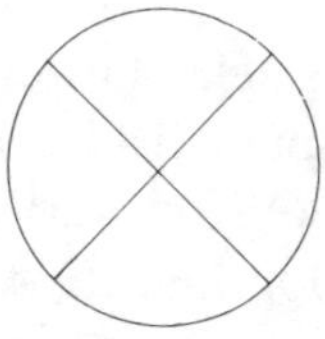
	An *Interagency I&R Subsystem* operates as an I&R department or unit within the host agency in which it is based.	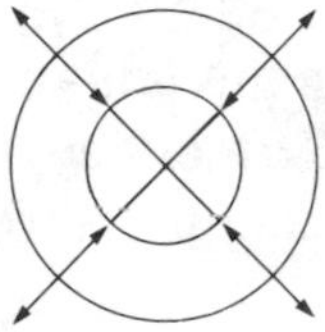
	An *Intra-agency I&R Subsystem* operates as an I&R department or unit that links clientele to other units of the parent agency in which it is based.	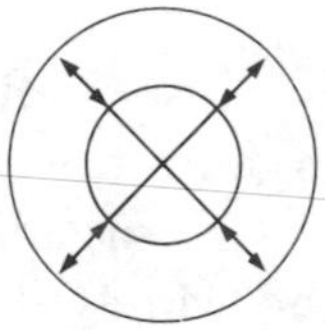
NETWORKS OF I&R SYSTEMS	A *Centralized Network* includes multiple I&R agencies in a designated service area that are directly accountable to a single generic I&R agency.	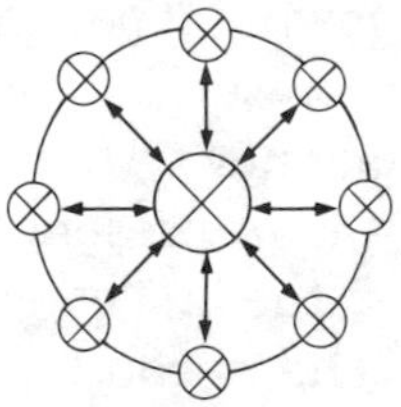
	A *Decentralized Network* includes multiple I&R agencies in a designated service area that may or may not link up with other I&R agencies.	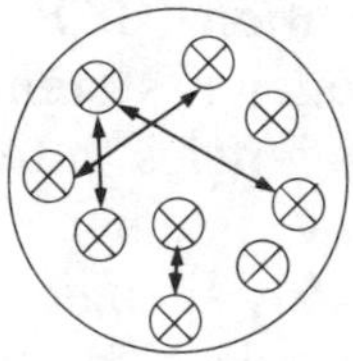

Key: X   I&R informational system
    Ⓧ I&R agency system

Informational I&R Systems

I&R service systems operate primarily as information and crisis intervention systems that transmit and impart information from various data bases through a variety of media, including telephone services, clearinghouses, published directories, radio, and television (both network and cable). The major means for communication in I&R services is the telephone. During the 1970s, there was a dramatic expansion of prerecorded telephone informational services relating to health and legal services. The fastest growing of these phone-based services has been Tel-Med's telephone cassette libraries on health care, which enable an anonymous caller to receive accurate, medically approved information by listening to taped messages on prerecorded casettes.

Tel-Med began in 1972 as an experiment in community medical information under the auspices of the San Bernardino County Medical Society. Within five years, over 100 cities had a Tel-Med program. According to Tel-Med (Tel-Med *Newsletter*, 1980), there are currently over 250 programs operating in 43 states. In fact, between 1978 and 1980 the number of users almost doubled and averaged over a million calls a month. The original tape library of 50 topics has increased to 335 tapes in the master library, many of which have been translated into Spanish.

To enhance and expand an operating I&R program, Tel-Med systems have also been incorporated in existing I&R programs. For example, the statewide information and referral system of the North Carolina Department of Human Resources, known as Call-Line, provides Tel-Med services as part of its I&R program on social services, as does Info-Line in Akron, Ohio. In Rhode Island, the Information Services of the Council for Community Services incorporated Tel-Med into its I&R system and has provided social work services on a 24-hour a day basis as a follow-up service to Tel-Med referrals.

A taped telephone message system referred to as Tel-Law has also been developed for legal information. Tape-recorded messages provide general information on the legal system and more specialized information on such topics as estate planning, adoption, bankruptcy, consumer affairs, separation, and divorce. A lawyer referral information service, which refers inquirers with legal problems to qualified lawyers through telephone-taped messages according to convenient geographic locations or by area of legal specialization, is also available.

One of the most important features of an I&R service is its capability to respond to crisis or catastrophe. Historically, the emergency conditions of World War II brought about the creation of Citizens Advice Bureaux in the United Kingdom, and in the United States veterans' postwar needs generated the emergency programs of Veterans Information Centers. As noted in Chapter 2, crisis information centers for drug and alcohol addiction and suicide prevention programs were among the earliest I&R programs.

To cover crisis calls that are received after regular office hours, a growing number of social agencies arrange to transfer callers to other I&R services that operate beyond the usual office hours. A popular type of crisis service is the hot-line, a telephone service that is usually staffed by volunteers who are trained to respond to emergencies. Hot-line staff are often composed of peer-group members, who are considered to have special understanding and empathy with the callers. The growing numbers of hot-lines indicate the pressing need of people in crises or perceived crisis situations to obtain information and reach care without undue delay. A hot-line request may entail a single contact or more extensive contacts between client and I&R agent. In either case, hot-lines rely on effective working relationships with other human service organizations to expedite referrals for what are often emergency conditions. In practice, hot-lines often tend to be transitory and may lack sufficient financial stability to maintain updated resource files and professionally trained staff to handle emergency conditions (Hyde, 1976).

Clearinghouses have become important information sources since the 1960s, when federal human service programs proliferated rapidly and often with nontraditional service delivery patterns. Clearinghouses may provide telephone informational services as well as published directories that inventory extensive volumes of human services. The *Catalogue of Human Services Information Resource Organizations,* published in 1980 by Project Share, consists of a list of 157 human service information clearinghouses, including descriptive profiles. The catalogue notes that in the process of supplying information, "resource finders" can also become the "solution givers" by knowing about and connecting with appropriate resource programs.

CONTACT Teleministries USA, an American affiliate of Life Line International, was founded in 1968 for the purpose of creating a national network of telephone counseling ministries. More than 80 CONTACT ministries in the United States provide 24-hour-a-day telephone help and counsel to lonely, troubled, and often distressed callers. CONTACT centers also sponsor telecommunications services for the deaf and hearing impaired and arrange for daily reassurance calls that are made to the homebound and to persons living alone.

To assist the consumer with inquiries that pertain to information on federal government resources, Federal Information Centers (FICs) have been established as a source of assistance to respond primarily to questions about resources that operate on a federal level. The FIC program was established by a directive of President Lyndon Johnson in 1965 and has expanded to respond to a wide range of inquiries that often pertain to veterans benefits, social security, immigration and naturalization, patents, copyrights, tax assistance, wage and hour laws, job information, and Medicare. Every state in the country has at least one or more FICs and many FICs work cooperatively with existing I&R agencies.

I&R Agency Systems and Subsystems

As noted in Figure 4-2, I&R organizational systems are classified according to their structural patterns as freestanding I&R agency systems and as I&R subsystems that operate within host or parent organizations. The interagency subsystem links clientele to resources within and outside of the host agency in which it is located, as distinguished from the intra-agency subsystem that links clientele to departments or units within the parent agency in which it is based.

Of the total number of agencies listed in the 1984 AIRS Directory (597), almost three quarters of the listed agencies (415) were reported as I&R subsystems, including both interagency and intra-agency subsystems. Of these subsystems over 70 percent

TABLE 4-3 I&R Systems and Subsystems Reported by Totals and Percentages

Types of I&R Systems	Reported Totals	%
Freestanding I&R agency systems	152	25.5%
I&R agency subsystems (interagency and intra-agency)	415*	74.5%
Totals	567**	100.0%

*Within the category of I&R agency subsystems, a total of 297 agencies (72%) reported operations in the voluntary sector; 118 agencies (28%) reported operations in the public sector.
**30 of the 597 agencies listed in AIRS 1984 Directory report no specific system or subsystem.

Source: Alliance of Information and Referral Systems Inc. (1984). Directory of Information and Referral Services in the United States and Canada. Indianapolis, In: AIRS.

reported that they operated in the voluntary sector under such widely diversified auspices as social services agencies, hot-lines, United Way affiliates, and self-help groups. In the public sector less than 30 percent of the total number of agencies (118) reported I&R operations within local or state government offices. Only 152 agencies, representing slightly over one quarter of all listed agencies in the Directory, identified themselves as independent, freestanding agencies (Table 4-3).

Freestanding I&R Agency Systems

The freestanding I&R agency is generally viewed as the ideal I&R model, since it is autonomous, nonpolitical, unbiased, and nondiscriminatory. While the British Citizens Advice Bureaux may come closest to approximating this ideal, the reality is that no I&R agency can operate absolutely independently. On the contrary, I&R represents an organization of organizations and is essentially an interorganizational phenomenon. For some community-based freestanding I&R agencies, local funding may permit considerable independence and control over their own decision making. The sources of outside funding often tend to determine the degree of independence with which an I&R organization can operate. While specialized I&R organizations, such as age-segregated I&R programs for the elderly, may tend to permit more independence than more general I&R services, the autonomy of the organization is necessarily limited by the inter-dependence of I&R systems with other service systems.

I&R interagency subsystems that operate within host agencies represent the most prevalent structural patterns of I&R programs. These I&R subsystems include agency intake departments, emer-gency services, crisis intervention centers, and hot-lines, as well as mobile services. I&R also frequently operates as an auxiliary service within a host social service organization, such as public welfare agencies, mental health centers, family and child welfare agencies, and other human service organizations. Reports in hos-pitals and schools also indicate increased involvement of I&R as a supplementary and complementary service to promote the pri-mary goals of health care and education in these respective institutions. While neighborhood schools, local libraries, and community hospitals have only recently become aware of the potential of I&R systems, linkages between these formal in-stitutions and operating I&R services have begun to be explored and merit further investigation (Levinson, 1979a).

An intra-agency I&R subsystem may operate in complex and multifunctional organizations for the purpose of linking con-sumers to resources available within the organization to maximize the agency's services. As described in a report on patient rep-resentatives at the Mount Sinai Hospital in New York City, the in-traorganizational I&R subsystem serves the total medical center by providing information and referrals to patients within the hos-pital system and by guiding inquirers to appropriate units within the total medical center. In the process of engaging in some lin-kages with community services, intra-agency I&R programs also tend to promote their own spectrum of agency programs. Beyond providing direct I&R services to patients and staff, the intra-agency I&R system may serve as an organizational quality control mechanism as well as a registry for organizational complaints. Ad-ministratively, the intra-agency subsystem at Mount Sinai Hospi-tal is conducted primarily by patient representatives with the cooperation and collaboration of the professional social work staff (Rehr & Mailick, 1981).

The intra-agency I&R subsystem that operates within the

Veterans Administration is also carried out by more than a single level of staff. Social workers in the Department of Medicine and Surgery and Benefit Counselors in the Department of Veterans Benefits are responsible for I&R services within the extensive health care system conducted by VA. As an intraorganizational system, a major aim of the I&R program is to maximize the benefits and entitlements available within the VA system and to establish liaison with outside agencies if and when possible.

The Public Library: A Dual I&R Subsystem

The emergence of library-based I&R services represents a unique combination of an interagency and intra-agency I&R subsystem. The I&R library program serves both the mission of the major library system and also interacts with outside service agencies in the community.

I&R programs within public libraries are relatively new and rapidly expanding subsystems. Library-based I&R programs are among the fastest-growing I&R subsystems and suggest vast potential for further expansion. The public library is traditionally revered in America as the storehouse of all recorded knowledge. Therefore, the current development of information and referral programs in public libraries is, in a sense, a logical extension of this tradition, particularly since the library is highly respected, apolitical, easily accessible, and generally available for services beyond the usual office hours of most service agencies. Library-based I&R programs represent an expanded service dimension for librarians, who by tradition and professional training are information specialists for all bodies of knowledge and for all information seekers.

The establishment of I&R services in public libraries needs to be judged by the recency and rapidity of its development and its enormous potential for growth of I&R services. It has been estimated that there are over 85,000 available public libraries in communities, public schools, and colleges or universities in the United States (Penniman and Jacob, 1984, p. 251). Prior to 1970 there is hardly any mention in the literature of I&R services in libraries. However, since the early 1970s, the development of I&R services in library settings throughout the United States has produced a rapidly expanding, highly diversified array of library-based I&R programs. Numerous acronyms have evolved to identify I&R library programs, such as TIP (The Information Place) in Detroit, PIC (Public Information Center) in Baltimore, NIC (Neighborhood Information Center) in Houston, and LINC (Library Information Center) in Memphis. Individual libraries and total library systems have implemented highly differentiated I&R programs with the support of federal, state, and local funding sources.

The importance that I&R is accorded in the total spectrum of library programs varies according to the historical development of the individual library-based I&R program and the level of involvement of staff assigned to provide the service. Budgetary allocations for I&R programs in libraries generally reflect the level of commitment of the administrative staff and the priorities of the elected or appointed members of the governing boards of trustees. A national survey of I&R in libraries (using a sample of 419 I&R libraries out of a total of 9,361 main libraries in the United States—not including branch libraries) indicated that the success of the I&R program in the public library is contingent upon endorsement from top-level administration and the commitment of library resources to I&R as an organizational priority (Childers, 1984). The emerging model of an interdisciplinary, library-based I&R program shared by both librarians and social workers suggests new opportunities for professional collaboration in I&R service delivery and the use of centralized data sources for community planning (NCLIS, 1983; Levinson, 1985).

Networks

A network generally denotes a constellation of multiple I&R systems that operate information and referral programs within a defined service area. A centralized I&R network usually operates a generic I&R program that provides a variety of I&R services to member agencies within the network. This organizational pattern differs from the decentralized network that operates independently and concurrently with other I&R systems within a defined service area. As noted in Chapter 8, many I&R agencies contain features of both centralized and decentralized systems. Serving as a generic centralized service to member I&R agencies, a network may provide a uniform classification system and a centralized resource for the collection, maintenance, and distribution of data that are shared by I&R member agencies. Through coordinated interagency programs that permit feedback of aggregated reports, opportunities for task sharing and collaborative planning are fostered between I&R agencies and other community resources. Because the benefits of networking have gained increased recognition as cost-efficient as well as service-effective measures, a variety of linkages of I&R systems has developed on all levels.

On the federal level, the Administration on Aging (AoA) has mandated the development of I&R networks to coordinate I&R services to the elderly on state and local levels. Spearheaded by the initiative of AoA, fifteen federal departments signed working agreements with AoA in 1975 and became members of a national interdepartmental task force to promote the development of I&R networks in their respective departments and coordinate programs on state and local levels. Members of the task force were a diverse group, representing such varied agencies as the Department of Agriculture, the Public Health Service, the Department of Transportation, and the Veterans Administration.

On a state level, Title XX of the 1974 Social Security Act offered state social service departments the option to operate their own I&R programs or contract with voluntary and private agencies. The result has been an expansion of partnerships and coalitions between public and voluntary agencies and the development of state I&R networks, such as the Info-Line in Connecticut and the statewide I&R system in Virginia. A 1979 report on Title XX services published by the federal department of Health and Human Services (*Technical Notes,* 1979) indicated that of the total funds reported for I&R by state public welfare departments, 76% was projected for state-operated I&R services, 17% for the public purchase of I&R services, and 7% for the private purchase of services.

I&R networks have developed along regional as well as state lines. For example, the regional Hampton Roads program in southeastern Virginia represents a combination of various counties, cities, and townships that are located in three planning districts. The parameters of I&R networks can be determined by geographic proximity, by funding sources, or by jurisdictional boundaries. However, I&R services that are restricted to the specific jurisdictional boundaries of cities, towns, or villages do not necessarily receive funding from these governing bodies. I&R networks have also developed in national organizations that maintain local chapters; these I&R programs are carried out at the local level by the organization's affiliates, such as the Easter Seal Society and the American Red Cross.

On the local level, 86% of the 597 agencies listed in the 1984 AIRS directory reported that they operate within the county unit of government. Fifty-five percent (330) of the reporting agencies restrict their services to a single county, whereas 31%, or 185, agencies serve a multicounty area. Only 39 agencies, which represent 6.5% of all reported agencies, restrict their I&R services to city boundaries. Statewide and multistate I&R operations include a combined 4.4% of all reported I&R programs, and a scant 2.8% represent other service areas.

The multifunction service center evolved as a locality-specific I&R service network during the 1960s. Some of these centers initiated I&R programs to help clients connect with an array of available services. However, since most of the services within the center functioned as discrete units, usually as outposts or satellites of larger organizations, I&R services have tended to operate without adequate coordination and therefore offer only limited access to available services. Nevertheless, the multiservice center represents a potentially effective model of a one-step center that is capable of offering a cafeteria of services to the inquiring client, providing a coordinated and well-integrated I&R network exists.

The effectiveness of networking is critically dependent upon the quality of leadership and the competency of staff in establishing organizational linkages. Networking is often a deliberate, sensitive political process of achieving effective working relationships among diverse agencies, each of which is interested in its own interests and organizational maintenance. Strategies for gaining support and creating viable I&R networks are discussed in Chapter 8.

COSTS AND FINANCING

While I&R services are usually free to all inquirers, the operation of I&R is not cost free. What constitutes adequate funding will, of course, depend upon the range, scope, staffing, and parameters of the I&R service.

It is difficult to ascertain the costs of I&R services in the absence of standardized units of services and centralized data reporting systems. A study by Hohenstein and Banks (1975) estimated that, according to empirical data, the cost per service request ranged from $3.50 in a metropolitan area, using a large number of volunteers, to about $34.00 in a small (ca. 125,000) community with no volunteer staff. The observed median cost per service request was established at $7.86. In identifying cost of I&R on a per-unit service basis, differential utilization of volunteer staff time is a critical factor. Are volunteers used as receptionists, resource specialists, or counselors? If trained volunteers are engaged in direct client contact, are the costs of supervision and training programs taken into consideration? In arriving at I&R costs, are the volume and type of requests handled taken into account? What in-kind benefits are provided by the I&R agency and other organizations? Are walk-in services more costly than telephone services, since more staff time is usually required to serve clients by personal contact? Interestingly, a 1975 cost-benefit analysis of case outcomes concluded that there was no clear evidence of significant differences in productivity or labor costs between walk-in services and telephone services. Another finding of this study was that, discounting the demand factor for age-segregated service and the possible administrative and political considerations, age-integrated services may be less costly to operate than age-segregated ones (Cooper and Company, 1975, pp. 178–179).

A review of 1977–1980 Title XX reports indicates that I&R funds are often subsumed under expenditures allocated for other service programs or absorbed under the general category of administrative costs. The difficulty of arriving at a valid cost figure is compounded by the fact that projected costs are often based on single I&R service contacts and not on an unduplicated count of individual clients. Based on the projected totals for I&R services reported by states in their comprehensive annual service plans (CASPs) for 1979, over seven-and-a-half-million clients were projected to receive I&R services in 1980 at an estimated expenditure of almost $117 million, a sum that represented 3.3% of all Title XX services. This estimated expenditure for 1980 represented an increase of more than $10.4 million over projected expenditures for 1979. From 1980 on there are no further data available on I&R expenditures under Title XX, since reported data were no longer published.

According to the agency reports documented in the 1978 AIRS directory, the major sources of federal funding for I&R programs were allocated under Title III of the Older Americans Act of 1965 and Title XX of the Social Security Act of 1974. Aside from the variety of evaluation and demonstration projects in the area of I&R during the last fiscal quarter of 1974 (accounting for $900,000), the Administration on Aging awarded $3.3 million to states to be utilized for I&R activities per se. A 1975 report by the United Way of America (*Community*, 1975) reported that local United Way organizations allocated almost $2.2 million to information and referral in 1974. This amount has no doubt more than doubled with the expansion of United Way I&R programs during this past decade.

Time-limited projects have often been terminated when federally supported grants were either depleted or withdrawn. This was the experience of the I&R project in Wisconsin (WIS), which produced extensive data during its operation in 1971 but terminated when federal funds were no longer available from the Administration on Aging. For example, the Neighborhood Information Center at the Queensborough Library was also discontinued when federal funds were exhausted after 1975.

While the development of private (for-profit) proprietary I&R services is limited to date, fee-for-service charges are attracting a growing interest. Contrary to the perception of I&R as a free service, the idea of fee-for-service charges, versus free, universal I&R services, is being seriously considered; the issue remains open to debate, particularly in view of budget cuts and reduced government supports. To date, the expansion of I&R services has relied heavily on adding or modifying existing agency programs to accommodate the operation of an I&R service. Cost effectiveness has been aided by reliance on in-kind benefits. For example, subsidies offered by computer companies have made it possible to computerize I&R programs, often beyond what I&R agencies could have independently afforded. The increased application of computers and other information technologies has generated new concerns over cost-benefits and cost-effectiveness. (For a more lengthy discussion of the costs of automation, see Chapter 5.)

Assurance of adequate funding for start-up and maintenance of the I&R service is critical to organizational survival. Many an attempt to initiate an I&R program has failed because of lack of adequate funds to meet the costs required to operate a projected I&R service. The majority of I&R systems are dependent upon multiple funding sources from the public, voluntary, and proprietary sectors. Federal, state, and local funding allocations tend to vary enormously from one fiscal year to another. A major source of federal funding for local library-based I&R programs has been Title I of the Library Services and Construction Act (LSCA), which is currently administered by the Department of Education but is allocated through state library agencies. During the 1970s LSCA funds were allocated for the initiation of library programs particularly responsive to the aging and the handicapped. A significant number of I&R programs in public libraries was started with LSCA funds, as shown later in Table 8-3.

A major reason for the expansion of I&R during the mid-seventies was the allocation of state funding for I&R operations and training that was provided under Title XX legislation. Since the release of these federal funds depended upon the budget projections of state departments of social services, as indicated in their comprehensive annual service programs (CASPs), the patterns of I&R funding by states have been grossly uneven, arbitrary, and often erratic. With the implementation of social services block grant (SSBG) legislation in 1981, which replaced the Title XX program, state allocations for I&R have been far more limited because of greatly reduced federal funding for all social services. Lack of standardized definitions of services and the absence of uniform reporting procedures have seriously compounded the difficulties in systematic fiscal reporting of I&R operations.

It is paradoxical that as federal and state monies have become less available for human service programs in the 1980s, the need for increasing I&R services has become even more urgent. A major impetus spurring the expansion of I&R operations despite the costs entailed is the rapid and dramatic advance in information technology and communication, a reality that is making I&R a growth industry of major proportions, as will be discussed in the following chapter on technology.

5 Impact of Information Technology

> "Most I&R services cannot use cost as the sole factor in a cost/benefit analysis to justify computerization. Improved service to clients and the community are the most important determinants in arriving at a decision to computerize."
> —William J. Garrett, *Technological Advances in I&R: An American Report*

The development of information and referral services during the past quarter century has occurred concurrently with the enormous advances in information technology that have impacted all dimensions of living, including the human services. New developments in communications have brought about worldwide networks of telephone systems, electronic libraries, cable systems, computer-based newsletters, and teleconferencing. Computers and communications systems link information systems that can share information with unprecedented speed and effectiveness.

While futurists suggest varying forecasts and different time-tables, there is strong consensus that our postindustrial service society is indeed an "information society." Bell (1973) explains that our intellectual technology based on information is analogous to the machine technology that characterized the earlier industrial era. Naisbitt (1982), in his study of megatrends, notes that we now produce information the way we used to mass produce manufactured goods. In a similar vein, but using a different framework, Toffler (1981) explains that information technology has brought about unprecedented information capabilities (the info-sphere), resulting from rapid technological progress (the techno-sphere), that have had a profound effect on all aspects of social living and personal lifestyles (the socio-sphere). Futurists tend to concur that the interface of the service society and the information society creates the potential for improved access to information capable of enhancing the quality of life.

As computers have become more affordable and more manageable for the uninitiated, and as information systems have become increasingly user-friendly, the utilization of computers in industry, government, and social services, as well as in the home, has created an unprecedented information revolution that has also impacted on I&R developments.

This chapter will deal with the current and potential impact of information technology and communications systems on various aspects of I&R operations—after a brief review of information systems that have evolved since the early 1970s to meet the everyday needs of all citizens as well as the specific needs of persons with special problems and concerns.

INFORMATION SYSTEMS

A 1976 publication of the American Library Association (Gotsick et al., 1976) on "everyday information needs for survival" lists such basic information needs as finding and retaining a job, maintaining a home, caring for children, keeping healthy, managing money, enjoying leisure time activities, and so forth. The rationale of this categorization is that "most people need similar kinds of information for preventing problems and/or solving them" (ALA, 1976, p. 3). While this statement may appear to be oversimplistic and global, the process of acquiring access to available information can be complex and may depend upon different motivations and individual skills in identifying, locating, and utilizing information. Childers (1975) identifies groups in the population whom he termed the "information poor." He found that it is primarily the economically disadvantaged who tend to be unknowledgeable, uninformed, and often overwhelmed with the complex procedures of procuring their rights, benefits, and entitlements. In contrast, the "information rich" are capable of utilizing available information sources that rebound to their benefit. How to facilitate universal access to information and services is a major goal in I&R service delivery.

Toward a Common Language

Information systems have to date been designed primarily for the convenience of the administrator or manager. More specifically, the technology of information systems has been used for inventorying the volume of users, maintaining quality control, and promoting cost efficiency. With the introduction of the computer in health and social service agencies, providers have established information systems primarily for administrative and managerial purposes, such as determining client eligibility and assigning fiscal accountability. Clearly, the operation of these management information systems has, until recently, centered primarily around the information needs of the organization.

Focusing specifically on the information needs of the consumer of human services, Bowers and Bowers (1971) examined client information systems. According to them, the term *information system* encompasses a body of organized procedures for identifying, collecting, processing, retrieving, and disseminating information centered on client services. They make a distinction between the information system that involves clients directly in the human service delivery systems and the more generalized information system that deals with the knowledge and means of gaining access to available human services. Operationally, however, an I&R information system combines both the service delivery system and the information system and follows through on referrals to other appropriate resources as needed.

In the overview and assessment of community information services in public libraries, Durrance (1984) distinguishes three kinds of community information: information and referral, local information, and public policy information. She maintains that greater clarity of I&R is needed and that more adequate preparation of community information specialists is essential to distinguish I&R from traditional library reference services.

To date there is neither a standardized method nor a central source for systematically compiling information on human service resources. Since the volume of services is vast and services tend to become highly differentiated, the available data on human services have limited consistency and coherency. The volume and complexity of human services data have pointed to the need for the systematized handling of vast amounts of information in order to carry out a responsible I&R service that is capable of connecting persons to available resources. For example, the I&R service in Minneapolis, known as First Call for Help, operates a resource file of some 1,500 agencies. In Baltimore County, the library-based I&R system maintains 2,500 entries in their files. The Information Center of Hampton Roads (ICHR) in northeastern Virginia has an information file that includes over 3,000 public and private agencies. A master file of 5,000 public and private community resources is maintained by the Community Resource Information Bank (CRIB) administered by the Los Angeles County Department of Public Social Services. In 1972, the Dallas Public Library began with 1,500 entries; by 1983 approximately 6,000 entries were included in the master file. Given the enormous volume of reported as well as undocumented human services, the need to establish a standardized resource information system is clearly a paramount concern in I&R operations.

The problems involved in arriving at the use of a common language remain unresolved and are compounded by the "soft vocabulary" that is generally used to describe social welfare services. Little progress has been made toward the development and acceptance of a standardized terminology. Achieving consensus

for uniform service definitions has presented persistent difficulties, since definitions tend to be ambiguous and overlapping.
For example, *long-term care* is not clearly differentiated from
short-term care and often depends upon the specific agency's
resources and the individual agency's mission. *Foster care* may include contact with natural parents or may totally exclude the
natural family, thereby restricting the definition to contact between the foster child and the foster family. Service providers
tend to define similar terms differently; for example, *counseling*
may apply to a single contact or to an extended period of treatment. On the other hand, the terms *hot-line* and *crisis intervention
services* may be used synonymously but usually reflect different
organizational mandates.

A national effort was made in 1979 by the Department of
Health and Human Services (formerly the Department of Health,
Education and Welfare) to explore the possibility of developing a
taxonomy of human services that could be used uniformly by state
and local social service agencies in their comprehensive annual
reports required under Title XX legislation. Despite the extensive efforts made by the Southern Institute for Human Services,
Inc., to arrive at a common language, no significant progress was
made. Long (1971) expressed doubt as to whether a standardized, national system of service definitions will ever be adopted,
arguing that the usage of terminology is a dynamic and continuous process of identification and redefinition that is inevitably subject to change in a rapidly changing sociocultural
environment.

Information Inventories

In view of the need for a central, national inventory of all human
services, it has been suggested that the Library of Congress serve
as a repository for systematically compiled information on available resources (Long, 1979). Lacking a national resource information base and a common language, various service dictionaries,
thesauri, taxonomies, glossaries, and lexicons have been compiled, all of which attempt to arrive at some logical and acceptable
approach to the categorization of services in a resource file using
a viable service classification system. The foundation of an I&R

service delivery system is the resource file, a generalized term that refers to a collection of recorded information with a common data structure that constitutes the data base. A community data base of services generally includes categories of broad general information as well as specialized information regarding social agencies, service programs, and service facilities. The underpinning of the data base is a logic and coherence that can promote effective data management in the compilation, storage, identification, and retrieval of data.

In terms of volume and comprehensiveness of required information, it is quite impossible for any one I&R system to cover all requests for information on human services. Limitations of coverage may be due to insufficient information or, conversely, information overload. Therefore the choice of data items needs to be carefully considered, with an aim toward a purposeful selection of relevant and useful data. It is helpful to formulate operational definitions for services that are listed in the service inventory. In order to enhance the utility of the resource files and provide consistency, detailed instructions for access and retrieval of information are necessary.

The data are generally organized and cross-referenced according to any of the following indexes: by alphabetical order according to the name of the agency, by type of service category, and/or by geographic locations. The alphabetical index includes all formally listed or commonly used names of service agencies, programs, or facilities. Each agency, program, or service facility may also be listed categorically and classified under an established service identification system, with code numbers assigned to identify the service program as well as the specific agency that offers the particular service. The purpose of the geographical index is to identify resources that are available at a convenient location for the inquirer. Varying geographical and jurisdictional units are used to specify service locations, depending upon the boundaries of defined service areas. Census tract data are especially useful to correlate client data with recorded socioeconomic and demographic data extracted from federal census reports. For purposes of standardized reporting, I&R service areas may also be organized according to postal zip codes, school districts, health planning areas, geographical boundaries, or jurisdictional divisions.

According to the 1983 national standards for I&R services (see Appendix C), each agency listing in the resource file should include, but not be limited to, the following descriptive data:

- Legal name of agency, address, and telephone number;
- Contact person or name of administrator;
- Services provided and identified by some uniform scheme;
- Application procedures;
- Fee schedule;
- Length of time on waiting list, if any;
- Area of service;
- Branch offices, addresses, and telephone numbers;
- Eligibility criteria (age, income limitations, insurance coverage, etc.).

The selection of the categories of information included in the working resource file will depend upon the volume of inquiries, modes of access, staff capabilities, the mission and resources of the I&R agency, and staff expertise.

SERVICE CLASSIFICATION SYSTEMS

The organization of a comprehensive and reliable resource file depends upon the application of a classification system that will permit ease in service identification and retrieval. Lack of knowledge and expertise in organizing a viable resource file may result in wasteful effort, even with a promising start-up. The range of information, the level of detail, and the technology involved in managing the storage and retrieval of information enter into the decision to select or adapt a particular service classification system. Experience has indicated that since considerable investments in time, effort, and expenses are required to organize and operate a resource file, any possibility to link up with an already established information classification system merits serious consideration.

While the classification systems that have been developed to date vary markedly, the three basic approaches of service classification systems relate to service goals, problem/service matrices, and key words and modifiers. The purpose of each of these approaches is to match identified problems with available and appropriate services. For purposes of discussion, these three categories of classification systems will be illustrated with a similar case example.

Service Goals

The earliest and possibly best known of service classification systems is the United Way of America Service Identification System, often referred to by the acronym UWASIS. The United Way originally designed UWASIS I in 1972 as a rationale for organizing and analyzing human service programs according to major goals in order to facilitate human services planning, programming, budgeting, and service delivery. Since the introduction of UWASIS and the reformulation of this classification system in 1976 as UWASIS II, many information and referral providers have used this classification schema as a guide to organize and access inventories of local services. Among the more extensive I&R classification systems that are adapted from UWASIS II are those developed in Hampton Roads, Virginia, and in Phoenix, Arizona. According to the reports on classification systems from the 616 agencies listed in the 1978 AIRS directory, over 65% used either the UWASIS I or UWASIS II classification system.

The basic UWASIS system is organized around six basic goals and includes 22 service systems, 57 identified services, and 171 programs. As shown in Table 5-1, the retrieval process begins at the goal level, then funnels down through the hierarchical structure of the service systems under which the identified services are subsumed, with further specification on the program level. A set of definitions for each category guides the worker in the selection of services and programs at various levels of specificity. It

TABLE 5-1 Service Goals

UWASIS—United Way of America Service Identification System

Goal III	Optimal health
Service system	Community mental health
Program level	Drug treatment

should be noted that the UWASIS system also provides criteria for measuring the effectiveness of various programs in the agency selection process (United Way, 1976).

The following example illustrates the application of UWASIS in a case situation involving drug abuse: A worker attempts to locate an appropriate service for a client who is a drug abuser. The worker scans the goal categories and selects Goal III, Health, since it is the basic goal most closely related to drug abuse. Following a deductive process in the selection of the service system and the service level, the worker then arrives at the program, Drug Treatment. Listed under this program are all agencies that provide drug treatment as defined by the UWASIS system.

Problem/Service Matrices

Though it is difficult to categorize the vast range of existing problems for inclusion in an information system, efforts have been made to develop codes for problem categories that are most apparent and most frequently encountered. The user inquiry form, which is usually designed to document the first encounter with the client, often requests a narrative statement of the problem, which may then be assigned a problem code.

One of the early efforts to correlate problems and health services was undertaken by Project SEARCH in Los Angeles County in 1972. The SEARCH system utilizes a matrix system that offers a cross-listing of defined problems and potential services. As illustrated in Table 5-2, the service categories are listed on a horizontal axis across the top of the chart and the problem categories are listed on the vertical or side axis of the chart. A glossary of terms has been developed by SEARCH to identify problems and services according to standardized service definitions. Entrance into the SEARCH system begins with the assessment of the client's problem by the I&R worker. The second step requires the worker's selection of the service category (of which there are 22) that most appropriately relates to the identified problem situation. The worker then plots the specific intersection of the vertical and horizontal axes on the problem-service matrix, which identifies an agency by code number.

Using the prior example of the drug abuser and his family, the

TABLE 5-2 Problems/Services Matrices (SEARCH)[a]

	Services		
Problems	01 Medication	02 Methadone	03 Home Care
Epilepsy (Ep)	Ep 01		
Drug dependency (Dr)		Dr 02	
Alzheimer's Disease (AL)			AL 03

[a]SEARCH: Comprehensive Health Problem and Service System, Los Angeles, California.

worker first selects Medical as the appropriate service category and Drug Abuse as the problem category. In matching this problem (on the vertical axis) to available services, Methadone Treatment is selected as the appropriate service (on the horizontal axis). The intersection of the problem and service items within the matrix identifies the agency that offers the most appropriate program (Cauffman, 1980).

Another major classification system (not shown in Table 5-2) that focuses more specifically on health and social service problem areas is the Louisville Human Service Coordination Alliance (HSCA) system, which categorizes services according to 20 major, distinguishable problem areas. The selection of the specific service is aided by a set of defined problem areas that can be related to identified services.

Keywords and Modifiers

In matching recognized problems and service categories, a classification system can also provide keywords or modifiers with which I&R staff can more accurately identify the specific services or range of services that are appropriately related to the particular problems presented. The specificity of problems and services is achieved by the use of key indicators or "discriminators." An early classification system that utilized this approach was the Information and Referral Manual System (IRMA) of New York City (1960), which demonstrated that, by utilizing service modifiers and facility modifiers, specialized directories could be produced for selected target populations (e.g., youth or the elderly) or for specific geographical areas within the city.

Referring again to the example of the drug abuser, a worker who wishes to locate health facilities in a particular geographic district that offers counseling and rehabilitation services for the drug abuser could select the major service subject area of General Health Programs, and the subarea of Rehabilitative Services. By utilizing service modifiers for Youth Services and/or Counseling and Drug Abuse, and applying facility modifiers for Location and Eligibility, the service program that best meets the requested criteria could be selected as the appropriate resource (see Table 5-3).

Another method of identifying resources is through the use of service discriminators (e.g., age, sex, income level, address) such as these compiled by the Network Exchange of Urban Services in Philadelphia (NEXUS) (Deahl, 1979). The computer reports the code numbers of agencies that can meet all the criteria in the search statement, and the agencies are automatically ranked according to geographic proximity to the client's address. Another example is the CALL file used by the Pike's Peak Regional Library System in Colorado Springs, which can be accessed by agency names, by 176 keywords, and by 154 cross-references. Keyword access yields the name of the service, a brief description, and phone numbers (Childers, 1984).

The first attempt to evaluate the utility and effectiveness of selected classification systems was Long's comparative study of six service identification systems (Interstudy, 1972). Subsequently, a more rigorous comparative study of four major classification systems was conducted by Haynes and Sallee (1976) in which

TABLE 5-3 Keywords and Modifiers

IRMA—Information and Referral Manual, New York, New York

Major service subject	General health programs
Subservice subject	Rehabilitative services
Service modifiers	Youth services, counseling, and drug abuse
Facility modifiers	Location, eligibility

classification systems were evaluated according to the following criteria: extent of flexibility, adaptability, and marketability. The introduction of increased automation in I&R services, allowing for more elaborate information systems, has resulted in the continued adaptation and expansion of some of these basic approaches to service classification systems (Garrett, 1984).

FILES AND DIRECTORIES

Directories of social services often represent the major contribution that an I&R agency is able to offer the community. Almost two-thirds of the 597 agencies listed in the 1984 AIRS directory reported that they publish their own service directories. Resource directories vary enormously in the range of entries and the scope of information reported on the selected services included. The well-known *Red Book*, published by the Community Council of Greater New York, has traditionally been regarded as the bible of services for New York City. This catalogue is organized according to functional categories of services, alphabetical listings of agency names, and geographical locations. The time-honored *Red Book* has been superseded by *The Source Book*, a resource directory of a new tri-agency coalition (the New York Fund/ United Way of America, the Human Resources Administration, and the Community Council of Greater New York). *The Source Book* has been prepared and organized for ready entry of data into an automated system. The data-base system, known as the Service Agency Inventory System (SAIS), consists of more than 2,000 organizations that deliver services in 4,900 locations in and around the New York metropolitan area.

To accommodate the requests of growing numbers of Spanish-speaking persons, the New York City library system produces an annual bilingual Directory of Services in English and Spanish. The New York City directory is produced through computer printouts and is published by the New York library system as a hardcover manual for dissemination to public libraries as well as to other interested service providers. Each local library in Manhattan, the Bronx, and Staten Island is required to stock an additional supply of other general and specialized published directories of social services to supplement the bilingual directory. (Queens and Brooklyn operate their own independent library systems.)

It is of interest to note that the Urban Information Center, located in the Monroe County Central Library in New York State, serves as the central information base for all I&R operations within the county. While the center does not offer direct I&R services, it publishes a semi-annual *Human Services Directory* in hard copy as a basic reference tool for subscribers, which includes not only public libraries but also churches, school districts, banks, and a wide variety of other I&R service providers. This directory is computer generated with on-line text edit and entry capabilities for instant updating. Another method for frequent updating was reported by Deahl (1979), director of the NEXUS system in Philadelphia, who described the ability of the NEXUS system to produce an affordable new directory every four months by combining word processing and microfilm technology. To enhance the accuracy of reported services and to provide service inventories in specific geographical areas, the Info-Line system in Connecticut issues regional directories that are compiled and updated by staff in regional offices and entered into the central I&R file located in Hartford.

Of growing popularity is the pocket-sized directory, or mini-directory, such as the one produced by the Community Council of Greater New York. This pocket directory provides a convenient information resource for emergency services and also lists major service organizations that are frequently used for referral purposes. A specialized pocket directory, called *Help Yourself,* was produced by the Community Council in English and Spanish as a guide for young people in New York City in 1985. These handy directories are particularly useful for members of the police and fire departments, as well as for volunteers, members of self-help groups, and community service organizations. It should be noted that the time, effort, and cost of producing directories have often been underestimated by the novice in I&R operations. Experience has indicated that the systemization of data on resource information and the application of appropriate technology to organize, store, and retrieve the available data can be very costly and time consuming.

APPLICATION OF INFORMATION TECHNOLOGY

I&R services operate at varying levels of sophistication, from shoe-box files to advanced computer-based systems. The organization, storage and dissemination of data require the utilization of information systems that can be easily accessed and readily available for information retrieval by either manual or automated systems.

In the 1984 AIRS directory, approximately 90% of the reporting agencies indicated that they operate manual I&R systems. Of the 182 agencies that reported the utilization of some type of automation, 104 agencies (19%) reported that their resource files are computerized. A smaller percent (13%) utilized automated operations to monitor client statistics, while only 10% of the total agencies reported that both their resource files and client statistics were computerized. In a nationwide survey of library-based I&R services conducted by Childers in 1981, only 7% of the libraries reported use of computer equipment for their I&R resource files; an even smaller number, 4%, used computers for information retrieval (Childers, 1984).

Manual Systems/Microform

Notwithstanding the growing capabilities of computerized operations, the traditional alphabetical card-filing system is still the most prevalent method used to inventory the resource file. Card entries are stored either in desk-top files or in floor units that can be operated as rotary or carousel files. The frequently used Roladex card file, which is usually organized according to the alphabetical names of agencies, offers ease in flipping cards by hand. The once popular McBee card, which aided selection of categories by means of inserting a metal rod through notched holes on cards, is infrequently used today, but suggests some of the basic concepts of an automated system.

Microfiche offers significant advantages over manual files in terms of economy of operational space and accommodation of information density. The space-saving feature of microfiche is that it can include a great deal of information on a relatively small card. Microfiche can reduce paper documents from 400 to 2,500 times their original size. Each card is copied onto a four-by-six card (a microfiche) that holds 70 to 350 documents. For example, the I&R system in Minneapolis, First Call for Help, reported that its system includes 1,500 agencies that are documented on 15 microfiche cards. In Nassau County, New York, 26 microfiche cards include a classified listing of over 2,000 service agencies within the county and related areas. The microform reader has the capability to enlarge the miniature film image on the microfiche to readable size. Duplicating copies of the original microfiche cards is a relatively simple process that can readily produce copies at a comparatively low cost for individual use by staff members. For purposes of economy and computer readiness, microfilm has been used as an interim step in transforming a manual system to a fully automated system. As reported by the I&R system in Phoenix, microfilm can also be combined with a computerized system for purposes of feasibility and economy (Deahl, 1979; Garrett, 1984). The computer-based directory produced by the Dallas Public Library combines an on-line automated system with a microfiche system for information access and retrieval (Childers, 1984).

Automated Systems

As consumer demands for I&R have increased and funds for service delivery have tended to decrease, the need for greater efficiency and time-saving techniques in I&R provision has become more urgent. Increasingly, agencies are not questioning whether automation should be instituted but rather when and how. One cost-saving approach to computer utilization is the time-sharing plan, which pays for a limited portion of time for computer operations provided by an outside organization. The I&R agency prepares the information for input into the computer; after the information is processed, the data printouts are returned to the I&R agency that has contracted for this service. An alternative to time sharing is on-line computer terminals that provide direct access to computerized data via on-line video-display terminals. These terminals are usually hooked into a central computer information bank for direct access and are strategically located in different sites within the I&R service area.

Advances in computer technology have led to decreased size of the machinery (hardware), reduced costs, and the introduction of new I&R programs (software). The large mainframe computers that first appeared in the 1950s have been replaced by smaller minicomputers and even smaller microcomputers. Nevertheless, the mainframe is still the major type of computer used for high-volume human service systems in which determination of eligibility for benefits is primary (such as the federal Social Security System, Medicare, and Income Maintenance programs in departments of social services). These highly complex computers require specially trained staff and tend to be expensive, costing from about $40,000 to well over several million dollars. On the other hand, the minicomputers are considerably less expensive and range in cost from $20,000 to $200,000. Operationally, the minicomputer usually does not need the temperature-controlled environment required by the mainframe computer, nor does it demand a very high level of trained data-processing personnel. The more recently developed microcomputer, also known as the personal computer, has gained increased popularity because of its smaller size and because it can be operated by nontechnical staff with comparative ease and with limited training. The comparatively lower costs of microcomputers, which range from less than $1,000 to $20,000, depending on their capabilities, put them within the reach of most fully funded I&R programs (Sullivan, 1979).

The amounts I&R groups can spend on automated systems vary markedly, depending on internal budgetary factors as well as outside funding supports. For example, the Community Service Planning Council of Philadelphia reported that in 1982 the cost of their automated system was $22,000 a year for time-sharing expenses and $8,000 a year for data-entry costs; however, revenue from directory sales offset some of these charges. The Community I&R Services of Phoenix spent less than $30,000 for all their hardware and software purchases in 1983 because of support received from the Honeywell Corporation. According to

Garrett (1984), the Crisis Clinic in Seattle is the only I&R service in the United States with a minicomputer dedicated solely to information and referral. The cost of their Prime 1000 computer, which operates with 12 local terminals and one remote terminal, is estimated at approximately $190,000, plus a software expense of $50,000. However, since the clinic received a grant from the McKnight Foundation to cover the purchase costs of all their equipment, the operating costs are expected to be quite manageable.

When is the appropriate time to automate an I&R system? According to Chapman (1983), the determination of whether automation is a practical approach to increased productivity is based on the agency's goals and objectives. It is difficult to determine the exact point at which the implementation of an automated system is economically feasible. When a disproportionate amount of staff time is invested in maintaining resource files and when record-keeping and reporting add up to a heavy cost factor, the consequences may be that staff resources are diverted from primary service-giving activities. As the volume of requests for services places more demands on limited staff time, a computerized I&R system may be an efficient and effective alternative. Since the costs of automated systems have been steadily decreasing, automation can be more readily justified, particularly when staff time expended on manual record-keeping may approach or even exceed the cost of automation over a given period of time.

It may be helpful to arrive at a decision on whether and when to automate after taking into account some of the following practical considerations:

Does the volume of data in the resource file justify automation for purposes of updating and storage?

Do the number of requests received, and the amount of information collected from each caller, require computer entry in order to handle the volume of transactions?

What are the number of variables that need to be cross-tabulated and at what level of detail?

How frequently do reports need to be provided on standard or varied formats, at what scheduled intervals, or on-demand?

With what frequency should directories be produced and updated?

How can the new technologies free up time for staff to work with people who need help face-to-face?

Weighing the immediate expenditures against the long-term costs and benefits is key to planning an automated system. Planning the manageable and cost-effective application of technology is usually a phased operation. Lekis (1980) outlines a sequential series of six steps in the implementation of an automated system that may ultimately lead to an on-line computerized system:

- Determination of a service identification classification system;
- Automation of the resource file;
- Development of computer-ready service reports;
- Design of selected data reports for planners, funders, and decision makers;
- Operation of computer remote terminals (CRTs) connected to a main computer system for updating and case management within a multi-user system;
- Communication through multiple interactive computer systems.

While Lekis (1980) recommends a progressive phasing toward computerization, she notes that *total* automation may be neither desirable nor necessary and that reaching any one of the above phases in computer readiness may in itself be a major achievement in attaining an effective level of operation. A practical, preliminary procedure may be to format data for entry into a computer system in anticipation of a projected plan for automation, as noted previously in describing the Service Agency Inventory System (SAIS), which is the computer-ready data base for *The Source Book,* the published directory of New York City agencies.

Regardless of whether computerizaton is involved, an information system must be continuously modified to meet the decision-making needs of an I&R agency. Consideration must be given to the development of an information system based on an assessment of staff preparedness and cost feasibility. After analyzing the existing information system and reviewing alternative systems, implemention of an automated system will require continuous testing and involvement of relevant agency staff. The conversion from an existing to a new system, such as transforming a manual into an automated system, can be fraught with problems, including staff resistance, operational complications, and lack of expert technical assistance. A rule of thumb is that all information systems require ongoing evaluation and modifications in the continous process of system improvement.

Combinations of technologies which are frequently used in I&R systems may involve the application of a variety of technologies because of financial considerations, availability of hardware, or time-sharing plans. For example, the Community Service Planning Council of Philadelphia computerized its resource file on an IBM 3033 through a time-sharing arrangement in which on-line editing is possible at the site of the time-sharing company. In Phoenix, the Honeywell Corporation provided the Community I&R Services of Phoenix with full computer assistance in 1978. The community resource file is stored on the Honeywell mainframe via a remote on-line terminal in the I&R offices. Information on resources is updated each month on microfiche and produced for sale to subscribers. The Honeywell system also creates a magnetic tape of the data base, which is submitted to a printer for the typesetting of a biannual directory of human service organizations. Currently, Phoenix maintains its major resource file on the Honeywell mainframe and an alternative resource file (e.g., church groups, local clubs, etc.) on its own microcomputers (Garrett, 1984).

The tendency in I&R automation is to proceed from less sophisticated unitary systems to multiple interactive systems that are capable of linking one system with another. For example, First Call for Help in Minneapolis developed its computerized resource information systems in 1973 on microfiche, with listings of 2,500 community resources that are updated on a monthly basis. A copy of the microfiche file and reader are located at the desk of each information and referral agent for immediate use in responding to requests from callers, and directories are produced biannually from the computer file. Both the directories and the microfiche are generated by first producing a magnetic tape of the data base that contains all the compiled data. When the Minneapolis I&R system received a $196,000 grant from the McKnight Foundation in 1984, the decision was made to convert the existing batch system into an on-line interactive system that can connect the data base of the Metro-Information and Referral Center in Minneapolis with the twin city of St. Paul (Garrett, 1984).

One of the major sources of resistance to automation is the fear of a digital society in which persons will be publicly identified by numbers and confidentiality will not be secure. The fact is that a wide variety of safeguards have been developed in computerized systems to protect the privacy and anonymity of the individual. While the procedures to ensure confidentiality vary considerably, the organizational policies of many I&R agencies specify security guidelines for the release of client information. Permission of the client must be obtained before disclosure of information is made. It is necessary to procure client consent each time information is released to an outside agency, with an explanation to the client of why the information is being requested, to whom it is being released, and how it is intended to be used.

The following report from the Hampton Roads Information Center describes procedures to ensure anonymity by obliterating client-identifying data over specified periods of time:

> The service record is not retrievable by name, but only by number. Certain records are singled out by an assigned number for follow-up (by random sample). All other forms are filed away by number at the end of each month, and not referred to again except to eradicate identifying information at the end of three months. Every three months, the name, address and telephone number of inquirers are purged by marking through with a black marker. However, records are kept for a three-year period in order to justify possible accountability requirements (Gilbert, 1975).

Other procedures to secure confidentiality may require that client data forms be stored in locked files and that access be restricted to designated personnel or specified levels of staff. Identifying information on the individual client may be stricly withheld from computer storage or may be accessed by specific codes known only to restricted staff members.

For reporting purposes, aggregated data on clientele may be used to provide public information without identifying the individual client. Clearly, agency policy must take into account the prevailing laws of the state or other ruling jurisdiction on access to privileged information and to client records. Under the regulations of professional licensure or certification, the conditions under which client records may be subpoenaed vary. When client information is sought by public officials, courts, or law enforcement bodies, legal counsel may be sought to clarify rights on disclosure of data. To assist staff in complying with agency policies on data sharing, a statement or manual on confidentiality procedures, reviewed and updated periodically, can conveniently serve as a common source of reference.

NEW CAPABILITIES

The early implementation of automated systems in the human services demonstrated that computer technology can promote greater administrative efficiency through use of management information systems (MISs). In I&R operations, data on services given, client characteristics, client eligibility, case dispositions, and budgetary allocations are systematically entered into MIS programs and retrieved for a variety of managerial purposes. MIS data have also been useful for planning programs and evaluating services. An added capability is the possibility of cross-tabulating service statistics with available socio-demographic data on client characteristics, such as specific age groups, income levels, ethnic groups, and housing conditions within designated geographical areas.

Perhaps the most widely acknowledged capability of I&R programs is the production of service inventories, which, through automation, can produce specialized directories from specific sections of the master working file or data base. For example, the I&R system in the San Mateo (California) County Library publishes a directory that contains about half of all entries in the master file; in Colorado Springs, the public library offers a complete printout of all entries in any requested portion of the total resource file. In Ontario, community information data bases and networks have been developed using an interactive videotex system that allows the user to select "pages" of electronically transmitted text for viewing on a standard television set. This videotex system, known as Telidon, permits its users to interact with a master resource data base and allows the transmission of text and the display of graphics using a telephone network with viewing capabilities added to the home color television set. Telidon is used by Toronto's Federation of Community Information Centers to create its own data bases related to local user needs (Bellamy and Forgie, 1984, p. 209).

An exceedingly helpful capability of I&R systems is the monitoring and inventorying of available resources through automated vacancy programs. In 1974–1975, Philadelphia developed an on-line computerized service registry designed to provide up-to-date, accurate information on vacancies in day-care programs, nursing homes, and low-income housing. A client could inquire about any one of these services, indicate preferred locations, and receive information on the level of fees and the mode of payment that was acceptable (e.g., Medicaid or Medicare). Based on the client's specifications, a list of agencies with available openings could then be generated. The Service Opening Registry (SOR), established in Philadelphia in 1974, was updated at least weekly, but was abandoned because the maintenance and updating costs proved to be very high and exceeded the fiscal limits of the agency's funds.

Unlike the Philadelphia vacancy program, which assumed total responsibility for maintaining updated inventories, the Crisis Clinic in Seattle relies upon the initiatives of interested service agencies for reports on their current inventories. The basic resource file can be modified to serve as a tracking system for vacancies in day-care and shelter facilities. Staff at area day-care centers and shelters bear the responsibility of informing the clinic when openings occur. Data on space openings are entered into the system and automatically removed after one week, thereby providing continued tracking and updating with minimal monitoring costs on the part of the I&R agency. The data retrieval system for this vacancy inventory is programmed to yield information on clientele, hours, fees, and geographic locations.

A relatively new area that is attracting increased attention in

I&R operations is the application of Decision Support Systems (DSSs) as an aid for professional assessments and case planning. Diagnosing clients and designing treatment plans based on computerized data is a new and challenging frontier in I&R operations. Computers have proved their importance in medical and clinical practices as helpful aids in arriving at medical diagnoses and treatment alternatives. The advances in end-user software and the growing interest in prototyping to simulate social service delivery systems have encouraged the application of Decision Support Systems by professional users. It should be noted that a DSS system requires technical sophistication and a recognition by professionals and administrators that DSS is a work-enhancing opportunity, and not necessarily a cost-cutting expedient. Licker (1983) points out that DSS can be helpful to the I&R professional who needs to access both general and specific data and make decisions in arriving at a plan for further action, including choices for referrals.

As previously noted in Chapter 3, an I&R service program represents an opportunity to participate in a planning process based on selected bodies of information that an I&R system is capable of generating. An I&R automated system can be especially helpful to the information specialist in locating needed services and can provide administrators with operational data for assessment and planning. In addition, other organizations engaged in planning may also be interested in the data products of an I&R system because of its capabilities to monitor trends and thereby establish documented needs for new programs.

While some I&R programs have accorded more importance to planning than others, it has become increasingly apparent that I&R reporting systems and interagency pooling can yield a wealth of data on services, clientele, and agency operations. Information on services provides not only an inventory of resources in the community, but also indicates which services are heavily utilized and which needed services are not available. By documenting variables such as total calls and/or total visits, the type of problem areas reported and referrals made, and the volume of clients accepted or refused for services, valuable information can be gained regarding the organization's capabilities and deficits in service delivery. Was the service provided or was the client referred elsewhere? When are most calls received? What is the nature of the presenting problems? Are requests focused on information only? Were the referrrals appropriate? Was another referral necessary? Answers to many of these questions may be found in the service statistics reported. I&R systems also offer the opportunity to systematically compile sociodemographic data on clientele organized according to age groups, income level, ethnic population, housing conditions, and by other salient socioeconomic variables. Documentation of clientele characteristics related to census tracts offers additional information on users when correlated with service statistics.

The I&R system operated by the United Way of Texas Gulf Coast is an example of an effective data retrieval system that uses I&R data for planning purposes. In 1976, the United Way of Texas Gulf Coast established an automated data system using a machine readable client case log form. The I&R system maintains a sophisticated on-line retrieval program on a IBM mainframe that is accessed via inhouse terminals. Workers complete one form for each I&R call, indicating the following information items for each direct service transaction: name, address, telephone number, race, age, and sex of client; problems encountered; referrals processed; time spent on referral and follow-up action. These computer-ready forms are completed by filling out various blanks on the inquiry form, after which the forms are read by an optical scanner. A variety of monthly reports are produced that include number of calls by problem areas, number of cases referred to specific agencies, demographic data, and follow-up on referrals that includes agencies referred to, actions taken, and documentation of unmet needs. The value of this kind of client data for funding agents, who require accurate reports on community resources and client utilization, should not be underestimated.

SOME LESSONS LEARNED

The reported experiences of various I&R programs reflect some of the difficulties encountered by I&R agencies in implementing and operating automated systems. The Community Service Plan-

ning Council in Philadelphia became involved with computerization in the early 1970s and initially attempted to make an on-line
computer system available for the I&R services of Philadelphia.
Although more than $1 million was spent on this effort, the sys-
tem never became operational. A major problem was that the
computer program that needed to be tested and debugged by the
computer consultant was not completed before the funding resources were exhausted. The shared administrative structure also
posed a potential hazard, since this project was jointly administered by the Community Service Planning Council and the United Way of Southern Pennsylvania. The dual organizational
structure under which this project was administered did not
facilitate timely decision making, thereby further impeding the
implementation of this overambitious undertaking (Garrett,
1984).

Various I&R systems have encountered problems of computerization due to the lack of well-trained staff and managers in
automated systems. Insufficient political support is another major
reason why I&R systems have become defunct, as was the experience of the Wisconsin Network (WIS) following the termination
of federal funds. The ambitious planning study of the Citizens'
Urban Information Centers (CUICs) that was designed for 187
library-based I&R programs in New York City branch libraries
was never implemented due to political strife and dissension that
prevailed during the early 1970s (Puryear, 1982).

Another reason for I&R failures has been the underdevelop-
ment of I&R systems to meet new and expanding needs. This was
the experience of the Information and Referral Manual (IRMA),
an I&R system that was initiated in the mid-1960s by the New
York City administration with a very limited staff. During its 16-
year history, IRMA succeeded in developing citywide microfiche
listings and computer printouts for each of the 59 community districts in all the boroughs of New York City. IRMA also developed
its own taxonomy of services through a grant received from the
Department of Health, Education and Welfare. However, by the
late 1970s IRMA was not meeting the needs of either the communities or the public agencies that it was primarily intended to
serve. IRMA gradually fell into disuse; since 1980, it has been
replaced by the computerized I&R system and data base of the

Service Agency Inventory System (SAIS), which was developed through the participation of 40 public and private human service agencies over an 18-month period (Garrett, 1984).

SUMMARY

The future of I&R and its relationship to the growing information society will depend upon the ability of I&R to apply the capabilities of information technology to the vast array of human services. A major goal is to enable the end-user to locate needed information as conveniently and expeditiously as possible. Ideally, information should be readily retrievable by user access, with minimal assistance from an information specialist.

The decision that administrators often face is not whether I&R operations should be automated, but rather when and how to apply the benefits of computerization to I&R systems. Rapid advances in the hardware and the development of new software to facilitate information management offer unprecedented opportunities to promote I&R operational effectiveness. Time sharing and cost sharing of computerized systems, plus the greater affordability of microcomputers, have expanded the application of automated systems in I&R operations. But the new technology is useless without trained human service workers who understand how to control, humanize, and harness the new technology to meet social service needs. Applying the capabilities of automation and information technology in I&R operations will in great measure depend upon the staffing and training of I&R personnel, as discussed in the following chapter.

6 Staffing and Training

"In a team effort, it is not necessary (or possible) for everybody to be equally good at doing everything, but rather, the staff as a whole will supply the balance of strengths required for successful operation."

—Clara S. Jones, *Training and Staffing for Optimum Service*

To date there is no prescribed nor ideal model for the staffing of I&R programs. Given the multiplicity of agencies and the myriad entries to services, the responsibility of meeting the service needs of all citizens appears overwhelming to any I&R staff. What constitutes an adequate or optimal number of personnel? The many variables that need to be taken into account in an estimate of adequate staffing preclude a predefined formula or an established staff ratio. A review of existing I&R programs reveals marked differences in staff levels and reflects a unique mix of professionals, paraprofessionals, and volunteers.

MULTILEVEL STAFF

Some I&R services may be provided by a single staff person who offers information and referral based on personal knowledge and experience. Other I&R services may be operated by a large staff that utilizes extensive computerized equipment. Some I&R services operate totally with a professional staff, as, for example, the Info-Line system in Connecticut, while other I&R programs are staffed predominantly by volunteers, as reported in the I&R program for the elderly in Humboldt and Del Norte counties in California. I&R agencies staffed primarily by paraprofessionals are often characteristic of neighborhood-based I&R services. More frequently, I&R service programs are operated by multiple levels of staff, including professionals, paraprofessionals, and volunteers, with different backgrounds and experiences and varying expertise. Required credentials also vary. For example, the staff of Info-Line in Connecticut is comprised primarily of graduates of master's programs in the human services, all of whom are hired on a full-time basis. The I&R federation in Los Angeles hires predominantly college graduates, while the Denver I&R program employs personnel who have completed high school.

Job descriptions tend to vary in accordance with the organizational mandate for the different levels of staff involved. As was noted in Chapter 2, American I&R groups initially developed specialized services that required staffing by professionals. Beginning in the 1940s, professional staff was mandated in federally funded I&R programs in the fields of health and the aging. With the advent of the 1960s and the establishment of antipoverty programs in local communities, I&R services were increasingly staffed by paraprofessionals and volunteers. The predominant pattern of I&R staffing currently reflects multilevel personnel who combine the talents and skills of professionals, paraprofessionals, and volunteers in varying proportions.

Volunteers

Volunteers constitute the core staff of a significantly large number of I&R programs. The role of the volunteer is particularly dominant in local I&R organizations that are associated with community church programs, hot-lines, and services to the elderly. Special interest groups, including women's groups, labor unions, and various health programs dealing with I&R relevant to such specific disorders as cancer, heart disease, and stroke, are frequently staffed by volunteers. National organizations such as the Volunteers of America, the Voluntary Action Center, and the American Red Cross rely primarily on the trained volunteer to staff their I&R-related programs.

A notable example of an organization staffed predominantly by volunteers is the network of British Citizens Advice Bureaux (CABs); the almost 1,000 CABs located throughout the British Isles are operated by a staff estimated to be comprised of 85–90% volunteers. Volunteers participate in a mandatory training program to prepare primarily for direct services in local CAB programs. The required training course for CAB volunteers is monitored by the central office of the National Association of Citizens Advice Bureaux (NACAB), which provides training materials and consultants to ensure quality training programs.

One of the unique features of the CAB is the volunteer solicitor, who is available for legal counsel to I&R clients by scheduled appointment. Town planners and accountants are also called upon to volunteer their services at the request of a CAB worker. The availability of legal counsel due to the no-fee policy of the British solicitor may also explain why CAB programs tend to assume a stronger consumer advocacy role than is generally found in American I&R programs. Although a recent waiver by the British Bar Association permits solicitors to contract with CAB users as private clients, the established rota system of volunteer solicitors still provides professional legal services to large numbers of CAB users who are referred by the CAB worker to the solicitor for legal advice, consumer complaints, tribunal representation, or legal redress (Brooke, 1972). While the British solicitor provides an impressive advocacy model in access services, it is quite unlikely that an organized plan for volunteer lawyers would be endorsed by the American legal profession for implementation in I&R programs.

Although the volunteer in American I&R services has been accorded a less prominent role than the volunteer in CAB operations, nonetheless the 1983 national standards for I&R emphatically state that "the I&R service should involve volunteers to enhance the program's service delivery" (Standard 17, Appendix C). Because volunteers are often acquainted with informal resources as well as formal services, and are generally knowledgeable about the mores, norms, and sociocultural traditions of the local community residents, volunteer staff can significantly enhance effective I&R delivery.

The stark realities of shrinking budgets and staff cutbacks that have occurred since the early 1980s have generated an increased interest in volunteer staffing. However, the recruitment and retention of volunteers are not without problems. The availability of the traditional volunteer homemaker is rapidly diminishing, as larger numbers of women are joining the work force. Volunteers are increasingly sought from the ranks of older citizens, particularly the retired elderly who wish to remain active in community services. The continued expansion of the Retired Senior Volunteer Program (RSVP), a federal program that is administered through ACTION for the purpose of volunteer services, provides a growing pool of older volunteers. Other sources for I&R volunteers are persons interested in a potential career in community services, including students in preprofessional training for such helping professions as social work, librarianship, nursing, teaching, and other human relations disciplines.

It is generally agreed that the volunteer can succeed only to the extent that adequate and competent supervision is provided. Limited supervisory time and inadequate training opportunities may seriously hamper or limit volunteer staff performance. Volunteer staff may also be restricted by professional biases against volunteerism in I&R services. Professionals may object to assigning volunteers to what may be considered professional I&R tasks. It is not unusual for the professional to view the volunteer with a mixture of suspicion and apprehension, since the volunteer may pose a possible threat of job displacement or replacement to professional staff.

Paraprofessionals

Paraprofessionals, who constitute a significantly high proportion of I&R personnel, are as much involved in administration and community organization as in direct client services. For many paraprofessionals, I&R work can serve as a career ladder and as an incentive to qualify for the human service professions. For other paraprofessionals, I&R has provided a full-time career, even without formal academic credentials.

With the encouragement of consumer participation in community service agencies, a corps of paraprofessionals evolved in the 1960s representing varying levels of education and diverse backgrounds. Much of the success of the local community action programs of the 1960s depended upon staff who were aware of service barriers but who brought to I&R programs a unique and intimate knowledge of the local community and its residents. The dual consumer–provider roles of paraprofessionals can provide first-hand information on the existing problems in the community and a knowledge of informal routes in gaining entry to local services.

Paraprofessionals have also been referred to as indigenous personnel, thus denoting neighborhood residents who work in local community I&R programs. It has been suggested that indigenous personnel have an advantage over professional workers in their ability to communicate more effectively with the disadvantaged groups in the community, particularly with the economically depressed. It has also been argued that indigenous personnel gain greater trust from clientele and are apt to be more partisan than their professional counterparts. Kahn rejected this allegation, insisting that "an indigenous identity has as many special pressures and built-in limitations affecting performance as a professional identity, without as many checks and balances" (Kahn, 1966, p. 66–67).

Ideally, I&R staff members will represent all groups and all income levels in the population. While ecomony in salary payments is undoubtedly a major reason for hiring paraprofessionals rather than professionals, the critical issue in differential staffing is the competence and ultimate effectiveness of I&R service delivery by each level of staff in accordance with appropriately delineated tasks.

Professionals and Professionalism

Professionally trained social workers were mandated in the federally initiated I&R programs of the 1960s that were designed for the aging and public health agencies. Many other professionals have subsequently become involved in I&R programs in a variety of different settings, including libraries, schools, hospitals, military installations, labor unions, rehabilitation centers, and other health and social service agencies. While I&R is generally regarded as a professional service, the professionalism in I&R operations is still not clearly defined, nor have formal accreditation procedures been instituted. The tenuously defined nature of I&R has led professionals to dismiss I&R as a given, assuming that I&R is an inherent responsibility of all helping disciplines. Moreover, professionals have been prone to regard I&R services as a less than professional responsibility and have therefore relegated direct service delivery to lower levels of nonprofessional staff and volunteers.

Another constraint is that many human services professionals view the new application of information technology in I&R operations with some misgivings. One objection is that automated responses to client requests may result in alienation between workers and clients. Another long-standing argument is that professional confidentiality may be threatened by computer operations. The fact that I&R professional providers are often not accorded due recognition in either status, salary, or career advancement has undoubtedly contributed to the limited participation of professionals in the development and delivery of I&R services.

Although helping professionals are aware of the persistent problems of access to needed services, may of them are reluctant to grasp the significance and potential of organized access systems. A major reason for this reluctance may be the uncertainty of their professional role. In fact, Long (1972) questioned whether professionals should be involved in I&R operations and, if so, in what capacity. His conclusion was that professionals should not be direct service agents but should restrict their activities to the tasks of administration, training, planning, and research. Kahn (1966, p. 66) also held that I&R services should be "professionally directed" and that professionals should provide guidance and supervision to paraprofessionals and volunteers; not, however, to the exclusion of assuming a role in direct client services.

As I&R programs have continued to expand and as requirements for technical expertise, supervision, consultation, program development, and interorganizational skills have increased, the need for well-trained professionals has become critically important. The knowledge base for professional preparation in I&R represents a fusion of experiential knowledge and theoretical concepts drawn from the behavioral, informational, and social sciences. Through formal and informal educational and training programs, this growing body of knowledge is being transmitted through formal instructional courses and in-service agency training programs. The publication of the 1983 I&R national standards and criteria for professional performance, jointly compiled by the Alliance of Information and Referral Systems, Inc. (AIRS) and the United Way of America (see Appendix C) has contributed to a clearer understanding of the professional conduct required for I&R quality service. As noted in Chapter 3, efforts have been made to establish a self-evaluation instrument by AIRS to provide a guide for assessing and improving I&R agency programs. The areas of self-study are based essentially on the 1983 national standards for I&R mentioned above and are considered to be the initial step toward accreditation. A significant benefit of accreditation will be the requirement for a professional review by qualified experts who will examine and monitor I&R programs to assure the maintenance of standards for quality services (Jacobson, 1986).

Recognizing that I&R is not the domain of any single discipline, some efforts are being made by professionals to engage in interdisciplinary partnerships, which tend to reduce professional competitiveness and to promote complementary relationships among professionals. Greater appreciation of the particular skills *of* professinals *by* professionals has demonstrated the value of tapping the specific competencies of I&R-related disciplines. For example, the Report of the I&R Task Force of the National Commission on Library and Information Science (NCLIS, 1983) strongly recommended that the human relations skills of the social worker can effectively complement the informational expertise of the librarian. Under a federal grant from the Administration on Aging, awarded to the Adelphi University School of Social Work in 1984, social work interns and library interns from the Palmer School of Library and Information Science (Long Island University, C.W. Post Campus) participate in an interdisciplinary I&R training project. The thrust of this project is to enable students from both professional schools to develop I&R services in selected local public libraries together with older volunteers. This I&R training program, which is targeted to services for the elderly, is identified as SENIOR CONNECTIONS. Following the initial grant from the Administration on Aging in October 1984 (Grant No. 90AT0126), subsequent funding from the New York State Legislature since 1985 through fiscal year 1987–1988 has expanded this program to additional libraries, utilizing teams of library and social work interns and a growing corps of trained older volunteers.

The cross-disciplinary nature of I&R, which extends beyond the institutional boundaries of service agencies, involves complementarity of functions and a recognition of the benefits of multidisciplinary and interdisciplinary relationships. For example, in assuming the role of an I&R intermediary, librarians have become aware of the junctures at which a social worker with personal helping skills and community organizational know-how can contribute to a more comprehensive I&R service, particularly in the interviewing process, problem delineation, referral methods, and the application of the professional helping relationship.

Through the operation of interdisciplinary I&R programs, librarians have also become increasingly aware of social workers' expertise in interagency relationships, community organization skills, outreach, and, where indicated, organized advocacy. Likewise, social workers have come to appreciate the informational and technical skills of the librarian and the opportunities for client entry and re-entry into service systems via a library-based I&R service. Quite logically, the library is a place to which a client–patron can turn and return as circumstance or change of condition may warrant. Similarly, librarians have come to realize that the social worker can follow up and retain accountability for service to the patron–client at various checkpoints in the service process at which the librarian may elect or be compelled to terminate contact. Thus, by working together, professionals can accomplish more than a single professional can achieve (Levinson, 1985).

In addition to the direct I&R service roles relevant to case delineation and case planning in which librarians and social workers are able to engage as professional partners, significant gains in planning and research can also be achieved through the sharing of a common data base of community resources. A common data base represents a rare opportunity for cross-professional pooling of information in assessing community needs, service gaps and inadequacies, as well as in projecting plans to reach the unserved and/or potential consumer. The complementary relationship that has been demonstrated between social workers and librarians can also be applied to partnerships that involve other professionals in I&R service delivery, including nurses, teachers, counselors, therapists, and other helping professionals.

However, it must be acknowledged that professional resistance and bias can exist and seriously hamper professional collaboration. For example, librarians may be reluctant to pursue complex patron problems lest they cross professional lines into the social workers' domain of diagnostic casework and treatment. Moreover, librarians have at times seriously questioned the appropriateness of the advocacy function in library-based I&R service delivery, asserting that advocacy may conflict with the neutrality of traditional library services (Gaines, 1980; Kopecky, 1972, p. 70). Rather than referring exclusively to published materials, librarians involved in I&R services may find it necessary to rely on nonprint information, a new and possibly unsettling experience for trained librarians. Furthermore, dealing with complex problems of the patron–client and handling personal identifying information in the referral process may be regarded by the professional librarian as inappropriate and intrusive. It is interesting to note, however, that Childers negated the alleged negativism of the professional librarian toward the social worker, by suggesting that "the great scepter of 'social work' may be imaginary and that experience may cause it to evaporate" (Childers, 1984, p. 46).

Similarly, social workers have also adhered to their own professional biases and have questioned whether the public library is an appropriate setting for personal helping services, particularly since libraries have been traditionally regarded as middle-class institutions that serve only the literate reading public and require a hush-hush atmosphere, preferably silence. Whatever reluctance exists on the part of professionals may be significantly overcome by a clearer understanding of the respective service roles involved in I&R provisons, as well as by the sharing of specific tasks by professionals in accordance with their professional expertise that is related to I&R.

THE I&R GENERALIST: A ROLE ANALYSIS

In order to optimize the performance of staff, it may be helpful to analyze the nature of the tasks and the roles assigned to I&R providers. As shown in Table 6-1, multifaceted service roles are assigned to service providers to perform various I&R functions. The seven major provider roles listed in Table 6-1 reflect the broad range of responsibilities included within the categories of direct and indirect I&R services: The information specialist, service intermediary, and case advocate are involved with direct services focused on client services; the class (or policy) advocate, administrator, planner/researcher, and educator/trainer are viewed as indirect service roles that tend to be agency focused. None of these roles is discrete or mutually exclusive; rather, they occur as combinations of interrelated roles. The specific tasks that are associated with each of these designated roles bear further examination.

In providing direct services to the client, the information specialist is held accountable for the delivery of updated information and the maintenance of systematically organized resource files. Information assistance may entail steering, which assumes that once the information is given, the inquirer or I&R user is capable of proceeding without further assistance. Should the inquiry involve advice giving or counseling, the I&R agent may enter into a process of helping the user formulate a plan or course of action. The I&R task may involve short-term counseling and/or referral to another agency, based on an appropriate professional diagnostic assessment. If the need for in-depth counseling is indicated, the service intermediary may supply a more intensive level of counseling or, more likely, will refer the client to an appropriate resource, as diagnostically determined. Whether selective or universal follow-up is provided will depend upon agency policy and

TABLE 6-1 Roles and Tasks of the I&R Generalist in Direct and Indirect Services

Services	Roles	Tasks
Direct services Primarily client-focused	Information specialist	Assist client with reliable and appropriate information from resource file and other data sources Referrals for specific information requests Short-term contact
	Service intermediary	Short-term and long-term contact Provision of in-depth counseling as indicated Monitoring referrals for complex situations Case management Interagency case planning
	Case advocate	Advocacy to assist the individual client and/or family through support services (transportation, translation services, escort, etc.) Advocacy focused on negotiations with other service systems in behalf of the individual client and/or family
Indirect services Primarily agency-focused	Class (or policy) advocate	Advocacy focused on aggregates of clients Advocacy focused on social action in behalf of a social cause
	Administrator	Intra-agency management (board, staff, client relations, community relations, etc.) Publicity, outreach, public relations Interagency linkages within service networks
	Planner/researcher	Participation in agency planning Community service planning Evaluation of service effectiveness Agency self-evaluation
	Educator/trainer	Staff development and training Staff supervision Consultation Public education programs

the provider's judgment of the client's readiness and capacity to follow up on a referral. Should the client be unable to follow through on the given information or the indicated course of action, the I&R provider may then assume the role of the case advocate in behalf of the individual client and/or the family involved.

In the category of indirect services, the class or policy advocate may undertake action in behalf of aggregates of clients who have reported a common problem or concern that requires public education, legislative action, or such adversarial measures as lobbying or public protests. For example, Detroit residents elected to raise their property tax to restore the hours of service in local public libraries as a result of a vigorous "Keep the Doors Open" campaign. Users of the library-based I&R services were organized and were among the staunchest supporters of the protest (AIRS *Newsletter,* 1984).

A key role in I&R operations is assumed by the administrator, who carries out the major responsibilities of hiring personnel and delineating staff assignments. Other vital administrative responsibilities include the ordering of program priorities and the implementation of organizational decisions related to staff operations and agency budgets, as well as the evaluation of I&R services delivered. Executive programming and planning involve relevant staff members and are shared with members of the agency board. Based on reported service statistics and data on community resources, the extent to which planning and research can be carried out will depend upon agency policy, available resources, and the commitment and readiness of the administrator and agency staff to engage in the planning/research process.

The educator/trainer is responsible for educational and training programs to enable staff to realize the agency's goals and to carry out the service delivery program. I&R agencies may have inhouse staff with the background, experience, and capability to conduct training programs. If staff trainers are not available within the agency, outside consultants may be engaged to provide the stimulus and expertise for staff training. The trainer may be an educator, a staff member from another agency, or a consultant with expertise in a particular area of knowledge or I&R skills. The consultant's expertise may be in direct service techniques (e.g., interviewing or role playing), in the handling of special problems (e.g., alcoholism or person-abuse), or in providing services to target populations. (e.g., women, children, or the aging). Essentially, I&R training is a continuous process that needs to be provided for all levels of staff in accordance with their respective responsibilities.

The comprehensive model of the I&R generalist encompasses many of the skills and competencies included in the roles and tasks of the I&R provider (as set forth above and shown in Table 6-1). Although each service provider approaches I&R tasks from a distinct and unique philosophical and ideological frame of reference, depending on training, background, and type of expertise, there are some common concerns that all I&R service providers share: notably, knowledge of community resources, skills in linking clients to appropriate resources, maintenance of confidentiality, and accountability to some official body as well as to the general public. What is suggested is a holistic unitary approach to generic and specialized I&R practice that combines both direct services to clients and expertise in policy, planning, and programming. The generalist, who is responsible for the meshing of service components for the individual and/or family, assumes a role that is comparable to the role of the general practitioner in the field of medicine. Beyond the concerns of the single client, the generalist also assumes professional responsibilities to groups of clients, while acknowledging internal organizational realities and external societal conditions.

While the social work professional has been an articulate proponent of the generalist model, reports on generalist practice are quite sparse. It should be noted that the generalist role is applicable to all human service practitioners (e.g., the public health nurse, the vocational rehabilitation counselor, the librarian, and the teacher). Quite logically, new curricula that view generalist practice as neither inferior to nor less demanding than a specialist program will need to be designed. Opportunities for I&R generalist practice will draw upon the flexibility and resourcefulness of I&R to develop innovative service programs in response to changing needs and new demands for access to information and services.

EDUCATIONAL/TRAINING PROGRAMS

While training programs for I&R services may differ according to the individual agency settings, goals, and resources, there are some areas of I&R training that transcend organizational settings and regional differences. According to a study conducted by McCaslin (1979) in Texas, differences in urban and rural I&R training programs reflect some significant variations, but the service needs perceived by trainees tended to be similar. Even for highly experienced staff, ongoing training courses in I&R expertise are essential to refine service delivery skills and maintain updated information on changes in policies, procedures, and relevant legislation. Training sessions usually deal with four major areas of knowledge and practice skills:

Agency services deal with the delivery of agency-based I&R services, including knowledge of information systems, use of the resource file, understanding of required documentation, and familiarity with agency policies and procedures.

Practice skills focus on the application and refinement of skills and techniques in I&R service delivery and case management, including interviewing techniques, problem delineation, follow-up, and case advocacy measures.

Policy analysis includes the acquisition of substantive areas of knowledge about the organization and delivery of health and social services relevant to policy issues, legislative mandates, information on pending legislation and changing eligibility requirements. It also includes awareness of service constraints, interorganizational alliances, and power conflicts.

Evaluation and planning entail the application of research skills in evaluating service effectiveness, assessing community needs and resources, and establishing bases for effective programming and rational planning.

In acquiring a thorough and intimate knowledge of the community in which an I&R program operates, information on the composition and characteristics of the resident population is vital, as is familiarity with the historical development of the community's services. Knowledge of current and potential sources of funding and financing is indispensable. Without recognizing the idiosyncratic features of the particular community and its social services infrastructure, a training program may miss opportunities to relate effectively to the specific needs of a given population.

Because of the need to be informed about services and benefits in a society in which the requirements for service eligibility are constantly changing, staff members need to keep well informed on policies and legislative provisions. Developing working relationships with legislators relevant to community needs and I&R services can be mutually beneficial. Training in outreach and public relations programs is vital to publicize I&R programs and to reach potential clientele.

In view of the new and unprecedented capabilities of information technology to promote the organization and delivery of human services, the I&R provider is not only expected, but required, to become familiar with the application of technology in I&R operations. In fact, without a knowledge of the current and potential capabilities of information systems, communication techniques, and computer technology, efforts to improve access through I&R may lag or operate with limited effectiveness. New demands for managers with technological expertise and professional experience in the human services have steadily increased. Among various reasons why training in the technology of I&R services has been delayed or neglected are the initial high costs of installing computerized systems, the limited number of staff trained in automation, and concerns about safeguarding confidentiality. (See Chapter 5 for a detailed discussion of these issues.)

In-Service Training

To meet changing needs and shifting service patterns, I&R training programs have developed a variety of on-the-job or in-service training programs. All staff in any I&R service setting, whether a social service agency, a library, or a storefront, require ongoing training in I&R expertise. Training programs should also involve support staff, including secretaries, who answer the telephones, and maintenance staff, who may respond to a phone call or a walk-in inquiry during hours when assigned staff are not available. Experience has indicated the advisability of offering training programs to administrators prior to staff training in order to familiarize them with the content of the program and to elicit their reactions and suggestions (Luck, 1976). The wisdom of initiating training with top-level management was demonstrated in an I&R project that sought to develop an I&R network within a cluster of health and mental health facilities. The need to gain the interest of top-level administrators became apparent when staff members appeared to be reluctant and even resistant to participating in the predesigned I&R training programs until the top administrators formally endorsed the program. Another lesson learned was that early and continuous participation of staff in the initial planning of the training program can significantly reduce the resistance encountered when staff are confronted with a packaged training program. The inclusion of staff in the planning and implementation of training programs can considerably mitigate against the not uncommon problem of burn-out, which may occur when staff are not sufficiently prepared to respond to heavy service demands, particularly in handling crisis situations.

Educational Programs

Some beginnings have been made to provide academic instruction in I&R in a selected number of colleges and universities. Varying educational and training programs designed to prepare professionals for I&R program development and service provision were introduced in a limited number of graduate programs in social work and library science in the mid-1970s. Several university programs developed field internships, research projects, and special curricula on I&R services. For example, the graduate School of Library Science at the University of Toledo offered a Community Information Specialist Program for library students interested in I&R community services. At Columbia University, faculty members from the library school provided instruction in I&R to both social work and library students under a federally funded program. Maryland, Syracuse, and Wayne State Universities have also offered some aspects of training in community information specialization. According to Durrance, a 1982 survey of library schools in North America revealed that less than 12% of responding library schools offered courses in community information services or specifically in I&R. According to the survey findings, "many library schools are not offering courses (in I&R) because they feel that there are no jobs in the field; paradoxically, a number of library systems and United Way agencies would be willing to hire such graduates if only they knew where such training was taking place" (Durrance, 1984, p. 63).

According to a 1986 national survey of university-based I&R/ Crisis Lines training programs, a total of 30 educational programs were reported by undergraduate schools and graduate schools of library and information science, education, medicine, and social work (Goldenberg, 1987). The Adelphi University School of Social Work in Garden City, New York, has been one of the few professional schools that incorporates I&R content in academic courses, field instruction, and research (Bucaro, 1980; Levinson, 1979a). As noted earlier, the Adelphi University School of Social Work, in collaboration with the Palmer School of Library and Information Science (Long Island University, C.W. Post Campus), is conducting an interdisciplinary training program that engages student interns from both schools, as well as older volunteers, in a library-based I&R program known as SENIOR CONNECTIONS.

Instructional Materials

Since the early 1970s, a growing literature on I&R has begun to emerge to meet the informational and instructional needs of I&R training. During the early 1970s, Long made a significant contribution to I&R training by editing a series of working drafts and prescriptive manuals on conducting I&R operations and delivering I&R services (Interstudy, 1970-1974). By 1979 various manuals and handbooks that dealt with direct client services and agency-specific procedures were being used in educational and training programs (see Coleman, Levinson, & Braverman, 1979). In response to the rapidly growing I&R programs in public libraries, Jones (1978) published a guide for librarians based on the I&R experience with the TIP (The Information Place) program in the Detroit Public Library. Focused primarily on training volunteers and paraprofessionals in a hypothetical, medium-sized urban community, Mathews and Fawcett (1981) offered some guidelines for staff training and program development.

One of the most popular and effective audiovisual aids frequently used in training programs has been the 1969 film *Tell Me Where to Turn,* which, though now outdated, was widely used for informational, instructional, and motivational purposes with students, agency staff, volunteer trainees, and community groups. A new videocassette on library-based I&R programs (SENIOR CONNECTIONS) conducted by older volunteers and student interns from library and social work schools was produced by Adelphi University, entitled *Ask Me* (1986). Other educational materials produced by SENIOR CONNECTIONS include a training syllabus and a volunteer handbook. As noted previously, the United Way of America published the first set of I&R standards (1972) and collaborated with AIRS in the 1983 publication of I&R standards (Appendix C). Roundtables, seminars, and training sessions on I&R are conducted with staff members of United Way affiliates. In 1979, a programmed resource and training course on I&R was published by United Way in the form of a workbook with an accompanying set of cassettes to guide the beginner in I&R operations. A newly produced videotape entitled *Reach Out* depicts a series of I&R programs conducted by United Way agencies.

A relatively new learning aid is computer-assisted instruction, which has proved helpful at the Crisis Clinic in Seattle. This clinic developed a unique feature within its computer system called *protocols,* which are detailed descriptions of services or problems to aid I&R staff in taking appropriate action. For example, when workers access the protocol on "poison," they are given information on the screen on how to respond to various types of poison situations. Emergency numbers are also contained on the protocol screen. These protocol screens are apparently useful for inexperienced staff and volunteers who must deal with crisis situations or handle complex eligibility requirements and application forms (Garrett, 1984, p. 191).

The quality of an I&R program hinges on the ability of its trained staff to operate a reliable and responsible I&R program. To meet the learning needs of the different levels of volunteers, paraprofessionals, and professionals, an ongoing program of staff training is indispensible both in the field of I&R practice and within academic programs that prepare practitioners. Among the various essential I&R skills to be learned and applied are I&R program development and effective networking, two vital areas that will be discussed in the following two chapters.

III Programming I&R: A Synergetic Process

7 Phasing I&R Program Development

"It is vital to acknowledge that successful system realization cannot be a hurried process. Much groundwork and dialogue must occur prior to the start of conscious system activities"
—James L. Shanahan, John J. Gargan, and Nancy Apple, *Building Model I&R Systems: A Bridge to the Future*

Diversity in I&R programs abounds. No one I&R program can be identified as a typical or ideal model. Until recently, only limited organizational studies have traced the origin and development of I&R programs. A notable exception was the four volume report on *Information and Referral: How To Do It*, edited in 1975 by Francis Gilbert, former executive director of the Information

137

Center of Hampton Roads in Norfolk, Virginia. This report suggested a three-stage plan for I&R program development: an initial
phase of study and design, followed by a second phase for the implementation and installation of I&R services, and a third phase
that includes program maintenance, modification, and evaluation.
Closely paralleling the phases of the Hampton Roads plan, the
United Way of America added a fourth phase in their plan for
program development, which also included program expansion
(1979).

Two recent and comprehensive studies of selected I&R programs reported on models of exemplary I&R systems and on selected library-based I&R programs. For the model study, seven
high-quality I&R systems were selected on the basis of defined
"criteria for best practice." Acknowledging that I&R systems
evolve in many different ways, the researchers of the models
study identified key stages in I&R program development that included problem identification, policy formulation, implementation, and evaluation (Shanahan, Gargan, & Apple, 1983). In the
study of selected library-based I&R programs, Childers (1984)
conducted a nationwide survey of I&R developments in American public libraries and focused on seven selected library-based
I&R programs for more intensive analysis.

Although I&R programs have evolved sporadically and often
with little prior planning, there are discernible stages or phases
that characterize I&R program development. It is evident that the
developmental phases in program development occur with sufficient frequency and consistency to suggest a sequential ordering.
For purposes of analysis, four distinguishable but interrelated
phases of program development are identified that are neither
discrete nor mutually exclusive:

- Planning and initiation;
- Implementation and operation;
- Modification and expansion; and
- Data utilization and evaluation.

Assuming an incremental approach in programming, it is difficult to establish definite time periods for the achievement of
program goals, nor can contingencies be predicted that will

either delay or accelerate any of these developmental phases. Before examining these four phases, a brief discussion of some of the catalytic factors that have generated I&R developments is called for.

MOTIVATING FACTORS

The start-up of an I&R program may result from a recognized need within a given community or from outside pressure or crises. A variety of motivating factors contribute to the development of I&R programs on all levels of operation. On a national level, I&R programs have been mandated by the Administration on Aging (AoA) under the 1973 amendments of the Older Americans Act. Under Title XX of the 1974 Social Security Act many states generated a variety of I&R programs through allocations for I&R training and program development within local departments of social services or under contract with outside agencies. In the voluntary sector, the United Way has historically promoted I&R developments through direct funding and technical assistance. The founding of the Alliance of Information and Referral Systems, Inc. (AIRS) in 1973 generated a broad national interest in the development, expansion, and professionalization of I&R. National voluntary organizations, such as the American Red Cross and the Easter Seal Society, have traditionally promoted I&R programs in their local auxiliaries. I&R programs have also emerged in response to local emergency conditions, such as floods, fires, droughts, and heating needs of the elderly during winter cold spells.

According to the findings of the I&R model systems study (Shanahan et al., 1983) the beginnings of I&R programs in each of the selected model systems studied had varied motivations, mixed staffing levels, widely diversified service boundaries, and different funding patterns. For example, federal funding from the Administration on Aging (AoA) promoted the formation of a joint I&R system in the rural area of Humboldt and Del Norte counties in northern California. AoA also contributed funds toward the support of the Info-Line system in Akron and the library I&R system (LINC) of Memphis. In the voluntary sector, local United Way funds encouraged the emergence and expansion of the evolving I&R network in the Denver area.

In the library field, grants from the federal Library Services Construction Act (LSCA) supported I&R developments in library-based programs, as reported by the San Mateo County (California) Library and the Jones Library in Amherst, Massachusetts. Political leaders have also fostered I&R developments in local communities through supporting the publication of I&R directories of community services and the creation of I&R hotline services. It is significant that in North Dakota the statewide I&R tie-line was established in the governor's office; in Connecticut the I&R program was initiated through a consortium of local United Way agencies and a newly formed state governor's council. On the local level, the library-based I&R program in Houston expanded to meet the information needs of city government. In response to pressures from constituents, city officials in Memphis released sufficient funds to support the citywide LINC system located in the city library system. Local taxpayers have also demonstrated that they have a special stake in the establishment of I&R programs that can effectively inform citizens of their benefits and entitlements. Assuming a strong interest and motivation in developing I&R services, the sequential phases of I&R program development begin with planning and initiation as discussed below.

PHASES IN I&R PROGRAMMING

Planning and Initiation

In I&R programming, the planning phase usually represents the critical first step in establishing a viable and effective I&R program. It is important to identify key community leaders, current and potential funders, interested groups, and members of organizations that may be likely participants in launching a proposed I&R program. Given the involvement of interested parties with a strong commitment to the establishment of an I&R service, the prospect of an I&R program will tend to attract other interested groups and community leaders. Exploratory meetings with interested parties may help clarify the needs, current resources, and the expressed reasons for the establishment of an I&R center. Contact with existing I&R programs or I&R-type services that operate in a given service area is an essential preliminary step.

Evolving from these initial meetings will be the likely formation of a planning committee with a charge to prepare a projected I&R plan. The composition of the planning committee should ideally include individuals representing a cross-section of various population groups and socioeconomic levels within the community, potential funding agents, and representatives from various human service agencies that reflect the infrastructure of community resources. Not to be excluded are representatives of community institutions that may elect to include I&R as a helpful auxiliary service to support and complement their primary services, such as the public library, the neighborhood school, and the community hospital. Interested local citizens can also make a valuable contribution to the Committee's deliberations. Gilbert (1975) suggests that it would be beneficial to include some "honest doubters" in the open community meetings to lend balance and to test the saliency of a projected I&R program.

The exploratory meetings of the planning committee usually reveal the prevailing level of interest and help identify potential participants in a projected I&R system. Given a working level of consensus, the committee will need to suggest organizational auspices, as well as determine the scope and level of projected services, the physical location of the I&R center, current and potential funding sources, and the goals and standards applicable to the projected delivery of I&R services. To guide the decisions of the planning committee, a preliminary feasibility study is usually undertaken by the planning committee members or by an appointed task force.

The Feasibility Study

Participants in an I&R planning study need intimate knowledge of the socioeconomic levels in the community, a critical factor in designing I&R services. Studies have shown that a client's receptivity to different entries to services may be related to income level. For example, higher-income groups are more likely to use the telephone, whereas many lower-income groups, and particularly the elderly, prefer walk-in services. While higher-income groups may readily relate to library-based I&R services, lower-income groups may prefer I&R storefront services. The geography and climate of the community may also reveal special service needs, such as information on fuel resources in cold climates and provision for emergency aid in areas that are subject to floods, hurricanes, earthquakes, or drought. The location of the I&R center may vary according to the density of the population in urban, suburban, and rural settings; it may also depend upon the availability of mass transportation. In the process of conducting a planning study, a review of the strengths and limitations of other reported I&R systems can be helpful. The choice of alternatives in program design will ultimately depend upon the availability of resources and a consideration of some of the following questions:

- Should I&R be a new service or an expansion of an existing service?
- Should I&R be organized as a free-standing independent service or as an auxiliary service?
- Which organizations or groups of organizations should be responsible for systematically maintaining and updating the resource file?
- What are the staffing requirements (either full-time or part-time) for adequate and effective service delivery?
- What is the anticipated volume of requests?
- Is the technology proposed for the specific I&R operation affordable, manageable, and efficient?

Some guidelines for projected program development may be found in an inventory of I&R services or related I&R programs that are already in existence, including generic and specialized I&R services. Of paramount importance are the information sources on community services that are listed for ready reference in local public telephone directories. Listings of community services in the yellow pages of the telephone directory are generally classified according to topical and alphabetical categories at a charge to the individual agency, whereas listings in the green or blue pages are usually provided by the telephone company as a public service.

In order to produce a comprehensive and accurate inventory of I&R services, a series of scheduled site visits to existing I&R agencies may prove helpful in determining the benefits or possible disutility of establishing a new I&R program. In addition to traditional social agencies, other settings for potential I&R programs may be considered, such as churches, schools, hospitals, libraries, banks, industrial organizations, and shopping malls. The extensiveness of the inventory of health and social service agencies within a given service area will generally depend upon the number of agencies, the geographic location of resources, and the staff resources available to conduct the survey. During the course of the planning study, special problems and concerns within the community may be revealed, and the extent to which an I&R program can gain political support may become evident.

In carrying out its charge, members of the planning study or task force will suggest a range and scope of services and define the functional levels at which the essential services of information assistance, referral, and follow-up will be provided. Support services such as escort and transportation services may be incorporated or postponed for future consideration, depending on apparent need and available resources.

In sum, an effective start-up for an I&R service will depend upon the reported findings, projections, and recommendations included in the planning study. The study may be conducted as a formal process, as occurred in the establishment of the I&R federation in Los Angeles and Info-Line in Connecticut. Or the planning efforts may be conducted informally as a consensus-building process without the benefit of extensive research, as occurred in the I&R networking efforts in Denver. Recommendations may include specific guidelines for implementation, as reported in the Los Angeles and Connecticut I&R planning studies, or first steps toward short-range and long-range I&R programming may be suggested in the development of a comprehensive I&R system, as outlined in a New York State study of 1980. Regardless of preliminary projections, various prerequisites must be met before start-up, such as the determination of governance, designation of auspices, assignment of staff, specification of data sources, and promotion of an outreach and public relations program.

Organizational Prerequisites

The appointment or election of a governing body is an essential first step in the initiation of an I&R organizational program. A board of directors or management board is usually comprised of community leaders, who are charged with carrying out the primary responsibilities of securing funds, approving budgets, appointing personnel, and generally maintaining the organization. Members of the board are selected to represent the geographic areas, jurisdictional divisions, and population demographics within the service area, including various socioeconomic levels. Recognizing the need for more specific professional advice and guidance, the board may suggest the establishment of a separate advisory committee.

The executive director, usually an appointee of the board, is the key person who is accountable to the governing board for the administration and management of the I&R program. The administrator's abilities to select and manage staff and to procure adequate funding are critical to the maintenance of an I&R program. In hiring staff, qualifications for professionals, paraprofessionals, and volunteers need to be defined according to specified tasks and responsibilities. Plans for staff training should be considered at the earliest possible phase of program development to assure adequate preparation of staff for I&R service delivery. Perhaps the most important initial task assigned to staff is the creation of an updated, reliable, and readily retrievable resource file, supplemented by other data sources.

The compilation and utilization of the resource file is a major responsibility of an I&R, since it represents an inventory of existing human services within a given area. Data that are systematically documented in the resource file generally follow a logical classification system for ease of data entry and for continuous inventorying, updating, storage, and retrieval. Since the resource file serves as the repository of community information data, keeping the file up-to-date entails periodic review and validation of all information. On-site agency visits, scheduled mailings for approval of agency listings, or telephone interviews can be used for purposes of verification and updating. Site visits are particularly helpful to obtain information on agencies that offer multiple services that require detailed service descriptions. Whether the updating procedures are handled in person, by telephone, or by mail, it is important to clarify the purpose for which information is being compiled and to explain how the data will be used. To keep abreast of the constant changes that occur in service provision, various published sources need to be consulted, such as newspapers, agency newsletters, government reports, and professional publications. Information on new staff appointments, changes in office locations, current and projected legislative provisions, and other service-related facts are often shared by professionals at official meetings and conferences, as well as through informal peer contacts. Quite often, information on new resources evolves from direct service contacts with clients.

For purposes of operational efficiency, the resource file need not be updated at a single specific point in time. A preferable practice is continuous updating of portions of the file at scheduled times, either by telephone calls to designated contact persons at agencies or by mailings of inventory forms to agency administrators, requesting approval of current entries and additional information on changes that may have occurred since the prior review.

In addition to the information available in the resource files, the following supplementary materials can be useful: telephone directories for specific service areas; service directories for federal, state, county, and local government offices; current rosters of public officials; census tract books and maps; city street directories and transportation schedules; ready-reference tables indicating eligibility requirements for such benefit programs as food stamps, medical assistance, and public housing; lists of law enforcement agencies; lists of emergency numbers and telephone numbers that are frequently used. Available information on resources for anticipated requests may also prove exceedingly useful, such as lists of nursing homes, licensed day care programs, sources for low-cost drugs, and lists of physicians who accept assigned payments from Medicare. Regardless of the apparent comprehensiveness of a published directory, there are usually informal resources that are not included in the printed directory but that may be exceedingly helpful and therefore should also be systematically documented for ready retrieval. In the final analysis, the translation of a request into an I&R service is contingent upon the information available and the competence and judgment of trained and knowledgeable staff.

An I&R service can be effectively utilized only to the extent that the public is informed about it. Use of radio and television as well as print media, including newspapers, eye-catching posters, informational pamphlets, special flyers, and billboards in trains and buses, are all effective means of publicity. Person-to-person contacts, door-to-door surveys, or street canvassing can also be helpful. I&R staff and volunteers may be assigned to strategically located sites, such as the local town hall, shopping malls, or the village square. Publicity at local conferences, conventions, exhibits, fairs, and special community events can help to establish the presence of an I&R program. The distribution of I&R literature to new as well as established service organizations can also promote and expand interest in I&R utilization. Whatever mechanisms or strategies are employed, an ongoing and energetic public relations program is essential to apprise the general public and potential users of the availability of I&R services.

Implementation and Operation

The second phase of an I&R program generally involves a process of routing the client from the point of inquiry to the satisfactory completion of the I&R service. This process from entry to exit has been variously called client tracking or case management, depending upon agency preferences and accepted terminology. As indicated in Figure 7-1, the process of monitoring the client through the I&R service delivery system entails the basic I&R tasks of information assistance, referral, and follow-up (described in depth in Chapter 3).

In tracking the client path through the I&R system (Figure 7-1), it is assumed that a reliable resource file is available and that staff are adequately trained to make sound professional decisions in problem delineation, in information assistance, and in referral and follow-up procedures. Figure 7-1 highlights some of the

FIGURE 7-1 Flow chart—I&R service delivery

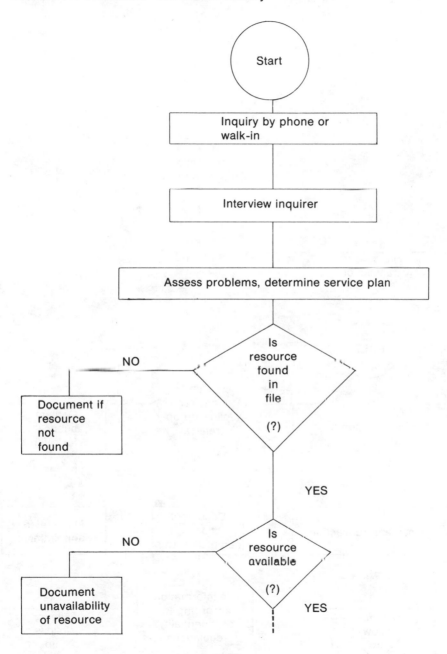

FIGURE 7-1 (*Continued*)

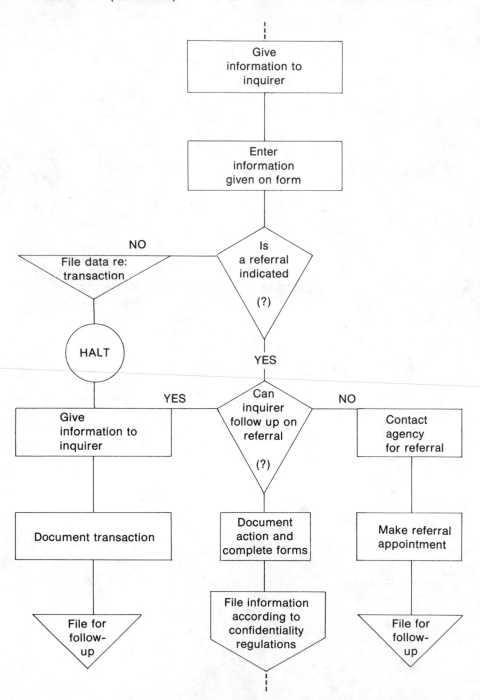

FIGURE 7-1 (*Continued*)

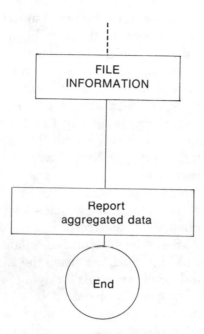

major decision points at which professional judgment is crucial: Is referral indicated? Does the client have the capacity to follow up on the information given? Is the referral acceptable to the client? At various junctures in the decision-making process either an affirmative or negative response is indicated, as a result of which different consequences inevitably follow. As shown in Figure 7-1, each transaction requires documentation of data, which are entered into a central data base for analysis and program planning. The record should indicate not only what transpired between client and I&R worker, but also the reasons the client cannot or did not accept a referral; the record should also indicate any gaps that exist in the service system. In the final analysis, the utilization of resource information and reported service statistics depends upon the systematic documentation of data by I&R staff.

As specified in Figure 7-1, information sharing and data reporting must observe the rules of confidentiality throughout the sequential steps of service delivery.

Modification and Expansion

Beyond the essential components included in I&R services, there is a wide variety of other services that may be added to or incorporated as a result of new priorities, emergency conditions, special studies, or new funding opportunities. Info-Line's six regional offices in Connecticut expanded their range of service capabilities by providing screening and/or intake services to various crisis intervention agencies, including the Domestic Violence Program, the Connecticut Prison Family Line, the Rape-Crisis Hotline, the Emergency Greater New Haven Fuel Bank, and the Hispanic Youth Crisis Center.

Another mode of I&R program expansion follows a complementary pattern whereby I&R agencies keep abreast of the range, scope, and changes in service programs in the process of providing needed I&R services to outside organizations. For example, the Hospice of Memphis, Inc., used the LINC I&R system to make effective and timely referrals for dying persons and their families; in turn, the hospice apprised LINC of the current resident population, the problems incurred in service delivery, and the possible need for other resources within the community. LINC's complementary relationship with the National Multiple Sclerosis Society has enabled the society to serve a broad clientele who may need I&R services that are not exclusively related to this health disorder.

A third type of program expansion is the incorporation of auxiliary services into I&R programs. For example, in recent years the Info-Line of Akron has expanded its services for older citizens by adding auxiliary programs that include Tel-Med, Law Line, the Emergency Alarm Response System, and MEDASSIST, a program for older persons who require medical services but who temporarily have insufficient funds to finance the needed health care service.

The capacities of I&R to expand and link up with new or existing programs reflect the flexibility of I&R to modify and mesh services in response to human needs. Table 7-1 lists categories of auxiliary services related to I&R that may be supplemental to or temporarily associated with I&R service programs. Under emergency services, I&R crisis centers may provide skilled counselors

TABLE 7-1 Selected I&R Auxiliary Services

Emergency services

Crisis centers
Emergency fuel clearinghouses
Emergency meals
Travelers aid

Informational services and counseling

Dial-a-dietician
Insurance counseling
Legal aid referral
Defensive driving

Seasonal services

Holiday gift clearinghouse

Registries and inventories

Homemakers
Live-in housekeeper registry
Nursing home registry
Volunteer bureau

Support services

Escort services
Telephone reassurance
Translation services

Specialized services

Teletype (TTY) services for the deaf and hearing impaired
Transportation for the handicapped

Source: Adapted from list of "Programs and Services to Expand Your Information and Referral Services." United Way of America. (1980). *Information and referral: Programmed resource and training course.* Alexandria, VA: Author.

for mental health needs, while emergency fuel clearinghouses may offer in-kind help to needy population groups. As shown in Table 7-1, I&R can also serve a public education function by directing persons to driver education courses or providing information on nutrition. An I&R program may also assign volunteers to schedule appointments for clients in need of legal services and insurance information. Maintaining registries and inventories of licensed nursing homes and matching homemakers with persons in need of home care may also be included in I&R programs. To overcome loneliness and isolation, home visits by outreach staff and telephone assurance services can be provided. As more I&R services provide teletype services (TTY), opportunities for the deaf and the hearing impaired to access services are enormously enhanced. The wide range of auxiliary services listed in Table 7-1 is not exhaustive, but rather suggestive of the almost limitless possibilities of I&R services to meet an apparent social need.

Data Utilization and Evaluation

Data that are compiled and systematized in I&R service programs represent a storehouse of valuable information that is useful for operational and evaluative purposes. In order to utilize data sources most effectively, it is essential to develop well-designed instruments and procedures that permit accurate and systematic documentation. The selection and level of detail of recorded and reported data are generally determined by the purpose for which data are utilized. Documented data from I&R reporting systems yield vital information covering some of the following areas of investigation: What are the nature of the inquiries and the incidence of problems presented? Which agencies accept or reject certain kinds of referrals? Do agencies restrict their services to a designated service area? Are some agency services overutilized in the community? Are some underutilized? What are the service gaps? Are newly arrived groups in the community familiar with and receptive to the I&R services? Are there groups of potential users currently not being served? What essential services are currently unavailable?

These questions are critical in evaluating I&R operations and particularly relevant to program planning. Based on reported I&R data, three sets of data profiles can be generated that deal with the characteristics of I&R users, the effectiveness of service delivery, and the assessment of community resources.

For optimal use of reported I&R data on clientele served, it is important to determine which items are of primary importance and which are relevant but secondary. In order to avoid collecting data that are either too voluminous or too scanty, forethought must be given on how and for what purposes the data will be used.

Client Characteristics

Data on inquiries and services given are usually entered on user inquiry forms that reflect the nature of the clients' requests, the problems presented, and the I&R service provided. In addition to documenting services rendered, the form should indicate if services are not available or ascertainable. Profiles of I&R users are based on the reported sociodemographic characteristics of the users, generally including age, residence, and ethnic group; if relevant, educational levels and income status are requested. Socioeconomic data on clientele may yield income levels, occupations, and employment histories. The extent of documentation on client characteristics will depend upon the level of detail required by the I&R agency for its reporting system. Based on systematically compiled data, it is possible to ascertain whether the reported users are among the population in apparent need of I&R services or whether the thrust of the I&R program should be redirected to reach a broader clientele or a different target population. It should be noted that there are two major difficulties in ascertaining client data: First, a significant proportion of I&R callers do not identify themselves and remain anonymous; second, I&R users are more often the initiators of the service and hence represent a self-selected population. It could therefore be concluded that the reported users of services are not necessarily from the population most in need of I&R services.

Agency Operations

A general practice in I&R programs is for each worker to maintain a daily log or tally sheet on all inquiries handled. By studying the volume, sources, and origin of the inquiries received, as well as the type of services provided (either directly by the I&R agency or through referrals), some understanding of the volume and quality of I&R services delivered by the agency may be ascertained. In addition to reports on the disposition of the inquiries handled (i.e., open cases, closed cases, referred cases, or cases earmarked for follow-up), client records may also reveal the agency's effectiveness or ineffectiveness in processing referrals of varying complexity. If inappropriate referrals are made, are particular staff workers at fault or does the resource file contain inadequate or inaccurate information? Can the amount of staff time required to respond to an inquiry be determined on a cost-benefit basis? Is an automated system indicated, and if so, what costs are involved?

Since agency reports are addressed to a variety of different audiences that may include planning bodies, community councils, and boards of directors, data are presented in different formats, such as statistical reports, analytical statements, graphics, or anecdotal vignettes of cases handled by the agency staff. Most importantly, the reports are intended to provide accountability to the agency's board of directors, to funding agents, and to the community at large.

Staff problems in reporting and completing required forms have often been attributed to the lack of cooperation of staff members. However, experience has indicated that staff resistance to documentation is more often due to lack of staff involvement and participation in the initial data selection. Other reasons for staff resistance may be inadequate instruction or insufficient sharing with staff of the purposes for which the data are being compiled. Regardless of whether data are entered manually or by computer, procedures for record-keeping must be clearly defined and monitored through on-the-job checkups and in-service training sessions. On a note of caution, the allocation of staff time for detailed record-keeping and extensive documentation should not impinge upon the staff time required for service delivery.

Community Assessment and Planning

Documented data extracted from user inquiry forms reflect the nature and incidence of prevailing social problems as reported by clientele. The extent and gravity of particular problems are reflected in the reported data on aggregates of clients. Problems may range from an immediate crisis problem, such as the plight of the homeless or flood victims, to problems of a more extended and possibly chronic nature, such as Alzheimer's disease, arthritis, heart disease, or other long-term disorders. Nevertheless, since social problems rarely exist as isolated phenomena, but rather appear as clusters of interrelated multiple difficulties, I&R data offer a first-hand report on their multiplicity, incidence, and gravity, as well as the availabilty and utilization of available services. Profiles of community services that reflect the range and scope of available resources are based on the data contained in the resource file. The effectiveness of I&R services provided to clientcle will, to a great extent, depend upon the efficiency of the resource file in providing accurate and updated information.

One of the major benefits of documentation is the application of I&R data to research, evaluation, and planning. Because I&R service systems reflect both demands for human services and first-hand information on the availability and utilization of reported services, I&R data are of special interest to funders and planners. While some authorities have viewed planning as a peripheral activity, the weight of opinion is that I&R data can be effectively utilized for planning agency operations, for designing and implementing service systems, and for promoting community service networks. According to Zimmerman (1977), provision for the systematic compilation of data for planning purposes should be an essential component of an ongoing reporting system and should, in fact, be established at the outset of I&R operations.

To foster closer communications between planners and I&R agents, Hansen (1978) proposed a unitary system of I&R data reporting that can serve the mutual interests of planners and I&R services providers. Based on shared funds of information that I&R reporting systems can provide, a common data base can spot service gaps, inadequacies, and insufficiencies in service programs; it can also provide valuable guidelines for policy decisions, resource allocations, and the internal management of I&R operations. As data-management reporting and data sharing are increasingly enhanced by computer capabilities, information on human services will become more readily available to larger groups of agencies for collective planning of health and social service programs.

In the 1980s, planning for human services has become increasingly urgent as restricted budgets for services have imposed tighter limits on service provision. On a sober note, Long (1971) is mindful that, notwithstanding the quality and sophistication of an I&R planning program, the political choices that determine service priorities and budgetary allocations tend to take precedence over more rational planning approaches. Nevertheless, the availability of systematized I&R data can provide an important and rational basis for planning in a society of boundless needs and limited funds.

SYNERGISM APPLIED

The key to I&R programming is putting it all together; that is, promoting helpful linkages in the interest of providing systematized access to available resources. In other words, the process of linking entails a synergism, which, deriving from two Greek roots, means "working together" ("syn" means "joining together"; "ergon" is defined as "work"). Applied to I&R programming, a synergetic process includes scaling and balancing I&R operations while allowing adequate time for the development of quality I&R programs.

Scaling

In view of the marked differences in size and scope of I&R operations, the scaling of an I&R program will inevitably depend upon a host of factors, including the funding, staffing capabilities, and the defined parameters of the I&R service area. Basically, an I&R program will be scaled according to its affordability and manageability given the current and anticipated volume of service requests and the availability of staff and other resources to carry it out. Initial considerations in scaling include the following: Who is the target population? What other organizations are involved in delivering I&R services? To what extent can cooperation with other agencies be achieved? How extensive should the resource file be? What essential service components should be included? What components are optional? Has sufficient staff time been allocated for follow-up services? Should the public relations program be limited or expanded to meet anticipated demands for consumer services?

Because of the need to allow for both anticipated and unpredicted changes and shifts within I&R programs, scaling is an ongoing process that requires flexibility and adjustments at any given point in time and is always dependent upon available or ascertainable resources.

Balancing

A critical question in operating an I&R system is how the multiple service components of information assistance, referral, follow-up, and advocacy can be combined to achieve an effective working balance. The answer does not lie in the equal weighting of all service components of an I&R program, but rather in the process of establishing coordinated systems and interorganizational networks that can achieve a workable equilibrium.

A balanced approach calls for allocating staff time for both direct services to clients and the indirect services that deal with planning, public relations, advocacy, and outreach. Extending services to providers as well as consumers and matching I&R tasks with the ability and availability of professionals, paraprofessionals, and volunteers require balancing staff assignments for current service demands with an awareness of the anticipated volume of services. In responding to the totality of human needs, balance in I&R services to meet the general needs of all users and the special needs of target groups is another essential aspect of synergism.

Timing

One of the major lessons of I&R programming is a respect for the timing and phasing required for sound program development. In outlining a temporal plan for achieving ideal I&R programs, both for single I&R centers and multiple I&R networks, Long (1973a, pp. 55–57) suggested short-range, intermediate, and long-range objectives. In planning initial steps toward the establishment of an I&R program in a middle-sized urban community, Mathews and Fawcett (1981, p. 13) estimated that approximately three months are required to start an I&R system and to train agency staff, providing a program coordinator can devote at least a half-time working schedule to develop the system. A more extended time period for I&R program development was projected by the researchers of the model systems study (Shanahan et al., 1983) who noted that it can take several years before significant permanent improvements in the performance of the I&R system can be realized. For example, the statewide Connecticut Info-Line devoted the first two years to developing friendly working relations with service providers prior to launching the first publicity campaign for the general public. The Los Angeles County I&R federation has been working with community entities and special interest groups since 1977 to develop a coordinated and feasible I&R system to serve the highly diversified, extensive metropolitan service area of Los Angeles.

Based on the developmental histories of selected model systems, the researchers estimated that the mobilization of interested parties, the drafting of an acceptable plan, and the preparations prior to the initiation of an I&R system may extend from one to three years, while the actual implementation of I&R activities may require a similar period of time "depending upon the expectations, needs and complexities of the community" (Shanahan, Gargan, & Apple, 1983, p. 4). These model systems analysts concluded that most successful systems are able to accomplish limited tasks in early implementation stages and make short-range improvements through interagency visits and skill-sharing activities. Longer-range improvements that begin early in the programming cycle include coordinated staff training, a standardized taxonomy, and a shared resource inventory.

Scaling, balancing, and timing in I&R programming are essential determinants of the scope and range of I&R systems that function within highly diversified networks. The following chapter describes the emergence and operation of selected I&R networks that have developed innovative and effective configurations of I&R systems.

8 Networking I&R Systems

> "If anything could be isolated as the most important factor in coordinating and integrating services, I&R is probably it."
> —Joseph L. Vigilante, *Back to the Old Neighborhood*

Dating from the early community-based programs of the 1960s, I&R has continued to expand rapidly and planlessly. The profusion and escalation of I&R programs that occurred without purposeful coordination during the past 25 years have led to a recognition of the need for interorganizational linkages. Consequently, diversified networks of I&R systems have evolved to overcome the fragmentation and lack of coordination in I&R services. The era of austerity and retrenchment of the 1980s has

159

accentuated the need for networking and interorganizational linkages.

Perhaps the best example of a coordinated national network of access systems are the CABs operated by the National Association of Citizens Advice Bureaux (NACAB) in Great Britain. All of the nearly 1,000 local bureaus are accountable to this national organization for certification, uniform standard setting and regulation, and devising training programs to guide staff in the use of a standardized, updated resource file available to all CABs throughout the United Kingdom. Unlike the British CABs, I&R programs in the United States operate with enormous diversity. In the absence of a national I&R policy and a national regulatory body, American I&R systems employ a wide range of strategies to promote networking. (See Table 2-1 for a comparison of the British CAB and American I&R models.)

Two decades ago, Kahn (1966) suggested the development of I&R networks, either under voluntary auspices or as combined networks of public and private agencies. Long strongly recommended a centralized, state-operated I&R network in his functional analysis of I&R in 1971 and in his classic study of I&R networking with diversified agencies in the state of Wisconsin (WIS, 1973). A feasibility study of I&R systems conducted in New York State in 1980 concurred with Long that I&R networking should be centralized at a state level for "developing, streamlining and coordinating I&R services through cooperative arrangements and interconnections." Networking on a national level was a major recommendation of the study conducted by the Office of Management and Budget, which advocated the organization of comprehensive, federally operated I&R centers to help overcome the gross disorganization and fragmentation of I&R services (U.S. General Accounting Office, 1978).

This chapter will consider two basic types of I&R networks: centralized and/or decentralized. Centralized and decentralized systems assume varying patterns of operation within designated service areas. A centralized network usually involves one major generic I&R system serving as the hub and providing support and assistance to other I&R systems within a given area. The decentralized network includes multiple I&R systems within a defined service area, all of which concurrently provide varying levels of

I&R services. A third network model represents a mix of I&R systems that includes features of both centralized and decentralized networks. Following a comparative analysis of centralized and decentralized systems, the remainder of this chapter will analyze a variety of strategies that tend to promote I&R networking.

CONFIGURATIONS OF I&R NETWORKS

In a sense, a network is a suprasystem that is related to formal and informal service systems within a given geographical or functional service area. Focusing on the network as the unit of analysis, Perrow (1978, p. 225) maintains that "we can best understand a particular organization if that is our interest, if we understand the network it has to play in." It is particularly important to know how tightly or loosely coupled organizational systems are and to know the interactions of individual organizations within a given network. The thrust of I&R networking is not to introduce completely new service structures, but rather to build upon what already exists by linking diverse organizations into viable interorganizational networks that can facilitate access to human services.

Centralized Networks

A centralized network is usually created when a single agency receives the major funding for I&R services and other agencies contract with this central agency for the provision of I&R services. I&R service delivery is thereby centralized within a single I&R organization, which provides centralized I&R services to member agencies. Figure 8-1 is a diagram of Info-Line, a centralized I&R network that operates in Akron/Summit County in northeastern Ohio. Info Line is the central point of consumer access to the human services available in the county. Through a cooperative relationship with its major funders (the city of Akron, the Area Agency on Aging, the county department of welfare, and the United Way), Info-Line is responsible for providing I&R services to other agencies (e.g., American Red Cross, the Arthritis Foundation, and the Akron Child Guidance Center) and main-

FIGURE 8-1 Centralized I&R network: Info-Line, Akron, Ohio, 1983

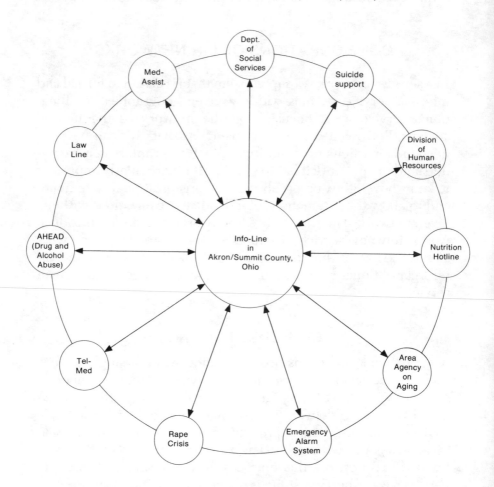

Source: Adapted from Shanahan, J.L., Gargan, J., & Apple, N. (1983). *Building model I&R systems: A bridge to the future*. Akron, OH: University of Akron Center for Urban Studies.

tains appropriate referral linkages with crisis intervention services and hot-lines (e.g., suicide support, rape crisis, the drug and alcohol abuse agency). Info-Line also assists other community organizations with support services, such as screening service referrals, handling applications for the energy credits program, and providing in-take for the nutrition hot-line. Info-Line has access to the United Way's IBM 34 for interactive access to the computerized resource file. As a centralized agency, Info-Line is involved with other programs that are targeted to the needs of the elderly, such as the Emergency Alarm System, Tel-Med, and Tel-Law, all of which are coordinated within the Info-Line network.

Decentralized Networks

Persons seeking information about needed services are likely to be confused by the existence of various I&R agencies that offer seemingly similar services within the same service area. Even within a moderately sized community, there may be an array of free-standing and agency-based I&R services, including hot-lines, crisis services, and specialized I&R services that are designed to serve particular groups or target populations. Some I&Rs may be autonomous; others may be subunits of multifunction agencies. Without a designated interorganizational system that coordinates the activities of these diverse agencies, I&R programs tend to be fragmented and often duplicative. The decentralized network attempts to provide some workable level of coordination between various agencies that operate on different levels of I&R program development.

Within the decentralized network, there is usually no single I&R that assumes total responsibility for conducting a generic I&R service program. However, one particular agency, such as the Mile High United Way I&R Services in metropolitan Denver, may assume the responsibility of developing a more closely coordinated I&R network. Interorganizational coherence is accomplished principally through cooperative agreements and informal decision making. A decentralized system may actually be preferred by local human service agencies that are uniquely suited to engage special groups of clientele who may be hard to reach through more centralized systems. Interestingly, the Mile High United Way I&R Service in Denver has developed a grassroots social service network with no public funding to support its I&R program. Figure 8-2 indicates the widely diverse organizations, representative of both the public and voluntary sectors, included in the I&R network. To promote the coordination of these various I&R services, the Mile High I&R agency has assumed the respon-

FIGURE 8-2 Decentralized I&R network: Mile High United Way I&R, Denver, Colorado, 1978.

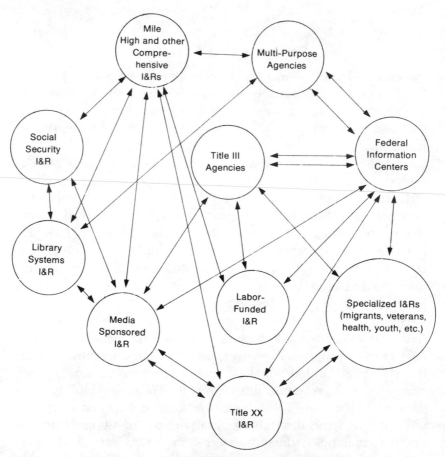

Source: Mile High United Way I and R Department, 1978, and Comptroller General's Office, 1981. Used by permission.

sibility of encouraging interested agencies to develop a long-range plan for a decentralized system of quality I&R services through voluntary networking. The intersecting lines on Figure 8-2 between the Mile High I&R and other agencies represent a related, but not necessarily coordinated, relationship. The varying distances of lines drawn between the various agencies denote differential relationships within the decentralized I&R network.

Centralized/Decentralized Networks

Although I&R networks may be categorized as either centralized or decentralized, operationally they reflect varying degrees of high, low, or moderate centralization and/or decentralization. For example, the I&R Federation in Los Angeles, established in 1976 as a major generic I&R provider, encompasses a broad array of specialized I&R programs. The Federation has recognized that the strength of these specialized I&R services is due to the extensive knowledge and particular skills that agency staff members possess in dealing with these specific consumer groups. The I&R Federation has evolved from a decentralized system into a more centralized generic system with a comprehensive, 24-hour service program. The Federation represents a primary I&R center and functions as the hub of an evolving centralized network that incorporates a vast number of specialized I&R agencies.

Another interesting model of a centralized/decentralized I&R network is LINC, a library-based I&R program that serves the city of Memphis and Shelby County, Tennessee. LINC is the central I&R agency that maintains communication with a wide range of public and voluntary service organizations. Organizationally, LINC is an integral part of the Memphis/Shelby County Public Library and Information Center. While LINC operates with its own staff and budget as a separate entity within the library, this I&R system also fulfills the major goal of the library as a comprehensive information center for all residents within the service area. LINC staff handles only inquiries that refer to human services; all other requests for information of a general nature are channeled to the reference department or other library services or appropriately referred to outside sources.

EXEMPLARS OF I&R NETWORK SYSTEMS

I&R networks vary enormously, depending upon many factors, including the level of community support, the resources available, staffing patterns, and the readiness of agencies to engage in coordinated activities. These marked differences are apparent in the two major studies, mentioned in the previous chapter, that reported on seven model I&R systems (Shanahan et al., 1983) and seven library-based I&R subsystems (Childers, 1984). (See profiles in Tables 8-1 and 8-3.)

Model I&R Systems

In 1981, the United States Administration on Aging (AoA) awarded a grant to the Alliance of Information and Referral Systems, Inc. (AIRS), to study selected I&R systems that represent models of "best practice." Researchers at the Center for Urban Studies at the University of Akron conducted a 17-month study, under contract to AIRS, during which they selected seven model I&R system that are essentially I&R networks. These exemplary I&R networks were selected on the basis of their capabilities to build strong linkages and develop effective interagency networks. The selection of the seven model networks was based on the following identifiable capacities:

- the capacity to engage in policy formulation and planning;
- the capacity to provide adequate resources for quality I&R services;
- the capacity to recruit, train, and retain competent professional I&R staff;
- the capacity to maintain and update a reliable resource inventory;
- the capacity to provide quality I&R to total populations in accordance with need;
- the capacity for organizational maintenance.

The model systems research team concluded that "most importantly," I&R must meet the need for a linking mechanism among a large number of complex and autonomous social programs (Shanahan, Gargan, & Apple, 1983, pp. 208–209).

TABLE 8-1 Profiles of Model I&R Systems by Location, Year Established, Service Area, Population, Volume of Calls, Funding, and Budgets

Title of I&R Systems	Location	Year Established	Service Area	Population	Annual Volume of Calls	Funding	Budget
I&R Federation (Info-Line)	Los Angeles, California	1976	County (83 incorporated cities)	7,500,000	265,000 (1983)	County; United Way; Dept. of Public Social Services	$1,600,000 (1983)
Info-Line	Connecticut	1976	Statewide	3,107,000	103,658 (1981)	Social Services; Block Grants (formerly Title XX); Mental Health; United Way	801,107 (1983)
Mile High I&R United Way	Denver, Colorado	1977	4-county region	1,620,000	29,903 (1984)	Mile High United Way	334,000 (1985 est.)
Info-Center of Hampton Roads	Southeastern Virginia (initiated in 1965 as a mental health I&R Center)	1975	7 counties; 8 cities	1,500,000	100,000 (1983)	Virginia Dept. of Social Services; United Way; Local Gov't.	340,000 (1985 est.)
LINC	Memphis, Tennessee	1974	4 counties (neighboring communities in Arkansas & Mississippi)	900,000	74,000 (1983 est.)	City gov't; AAA; Revenue sharing	180,000 (1983)
Info-Line	Akron, Ohio	1976	1 county	520,000	105,872 (1983 est.)	City of Akron; Agency of Aging; Dept. of Welfare; United Way Others	285,400 (1983)
Humboldt/ Del Norte I&R System	Humboldt & Del Norte California	1980	2 counties	126,731	9,671 (1983)	AAA; pvt. foundation	63,654 (1983)

Source: *Model Information and Referral Systems: A Bridge to the Future.* A comparative report by James L. Shanahan, John J. Gargan, and Nancy Apple, 1983. Alliance of Information and Referral Systems, Inc. Akron, Ohio: University of Akron Center for Urban Studies.

The model systems report noted that within the service areas of the seven model systems, some means of access to services exist, some level of funding is operative, and some form of resource inventory is maintained. However, as noted on Table 8-1, there are marked differences between the service areas in geographical boundaries, jurisdictional divisions, and population size. Whereas the I&R Federation in Los Angeles is essentially urban, the I&R program in Humboldt and Del Norte counties in northern California is primarily rural. I&R networks in Connecticut and southeastern Virginia include both urban and rural constituencies. As reported in the model systems study (Shanahan et al., 1983), the population within service areas ranges from approximately 125,000 in the bicounty service area in rural California to more than 7 million in the Los Angeles I&R Federation network. In contrast to the statewide Connecticut I&R network, which operates through its six regional offices, the I&R network in South Dakota, a large rural state with a small population, operates primarily through its central, statewide telephone tie-line (Goodroad, 1980). A recent study of rural I&R services for the elderly has indicated that I&R networking can be helpful in reaching limited resources and overcoming distance problems with the aid of trained volunteer staff (Ernst, 1981). Rather than operating from an established office location, an I&R network may conduct a mobile service that brings its services to inquirers at various locations; for example, the Wire Van Service in Boston or the Senior Mobile in Nassau County, New York.

Formal or informal modes of networking often depend upon the tradition or historical experience of a given service area. For example, I&R developments in Denver have traditionally followed a personalized grassroots approach. Similarly, the I&R network that exists in Humboldt and Del Norte counties in California operates primarily within a folksy, informal climate. In contrast, the statewide Info-Line in Connecticut and the LINC system in metropolitan Memphis maintain formal relationships with state and city governments.

Service areas may also operate at various hierarchical levels. As seen in Table 8-1, I&R service areas are comprised of different combinations of cities, counties, and regions that are inhabited by varying sizes of population. For example, the Info-Line system in

Connecticut, which was initially organized as a statewide system, operates through regional offices in the absence of clearly defined county units. Unlike the Connecticut Info-Line, which was initially organized on a state level, Virginia arrived at its statewide system through the leadership of one of its regional planning areas, the Information Center of Hampton Roads in southeastern Virginia, which served as a prototype for other regional areas in the state.

It is interesting to note that some I&R systems extend their services beyond their respective state borders. In Memphis, for example, the LINC system delivers I&R services in neighboring communities in Arkansas and Mississippi. Regional I&R systems may also go beyond state boundaries, as does the Voluntary Action and Information Center in Kansas City, which serves the bi-state area of Missouri and Kansas. Most I&R services, however, are organized at single- or multicounty levels. Info-Line in Akron, which is located in Summit County, serves only the urban area of a single county, whereas Humboldt and Del Norte counties are combined in a single rural service area. In the Denver area, the boundaries of the Mile High I&R system encompass a four-county area.

As noted in Table 8-2, the volume of calls reported may or may not have a relationship to the total population of the service area. For example, the Akron Info-Line and Information Center of Hampton Roads reported a similar number of calls in 1983, even though the Hampton Roads service area included almost three times the population of Akron. Significantly, the Denver I&R system reported less than one-third of the number of calls as Hampton Roads, despite a slightly larger population. The LINC system in Memphis serves almost twice the total population of Akron, but the Akron Info-Line recorded more than double the number of calls in 1983.

In terms of rank order, the I&R Federation in Los Angeles is highest in both population size and number of calls reported. The Information Center of the Hampton Roads and the LINC system in Memphis ranked fourth and fifth, both in total population and the number of calls. In contrast, Info-Line in Akron reported the second highest number of calls but ranked sixth in total population.

TABLE 8-2 Ranking of Model I&R Systems by Population and Volume of Calls

Site of Model Systems	Rank by Population	Rank by Volume of Calls
I&R Federation of Los Angeles (INFO LINE)	1	1
Info-Line, Connecticut	2	3
Mile High United Way, Denver	3	6
Information Center of Hampton Roads, southeastern Virginia	4	4
LINC, Memphis	5	5
Info-Line, Akron	6	2
Humboldt/Del Norte, California	7	7

Shanahan, J.L., Gargan, J.J., & Apple, N. (1983). *Model information and referral systems: A Bridge to the future.* Alliance of Information and Referral Systems, Inc. Akron, Ohio: University of Akron Center for Urban Studies.

Multiple funding sources from both the public and voluntary sectors support five of the seven reported I&R model programs. In Denver, the Mile High United Way relies almost exclusively on the voluntary funding of United Way, whereas in Memphis, city funds are the primary source of support for the LINC I&R network. A trend of fiscal support from the private, profit-making sector is evident. For example, the referral agent program in Denver has been implemented in various corporations that have made substantial contributions to United Way. In the referral agent program, corporate funds support I&R programs that are conducted by employees trained as I&R agents by the United Way (Shanahan et al., 1983). In Humboldt and Del Norte counties in California, a private foundation contributes to the support of this I&R system, as does the Area Agency on Aging. It is of interest to note that this bicounty network represents the only age-specific model I&R program; the other six model I&R systems provide generic I&R services.

Library-Based I&R Subsystems

The seven libraries in the Childers (1984) survey represent unique variations in the development and operation of these library-based I&R programs. The determining criteria for selection were a representation of differences in locale or setting, the nature of the clientele, the use of manual or computer-based operations, the branch libraries involved, and the role of I&R, both as a direct service and a support service to other agencies (Table 8-3). It is significant that the LINC system in Memphis, which was selected as a model system in the AIRS study, was also included as a library site in the library survey report. Interestingly, Childers (1984, p. 217) observes that "in Memphis, the innovation (I&R) moved forward on the grandest scale of any site."

Some library-based I&R services engage in significant networking with other agencies. For example, in San Mateo County (California), an information consortium (ICON) consists of social workers, probation officers, and educators as well as librarians. Since the beginning of its I&R program, the Baltimore County Public Library has cooperated closely with the city's Health and Welfare Council I&R service. Thus, the I&R library-based subsystem constitutes a network within the total library system and its branches and within the larger network of I&R services in the community.

The seven libraries selected in the Childers survey reflect a variety of designated service areas, including library sites within urban settings (Dallas and Pike's Peak), suburban settings (Baltimore County and San Mateo County), and rural settings (Amherst and Caroline Counties). Interestingly, the LINC system in Memphis encompasses urban, suburban, and rural regions within the defined areas that are served by LINC. Except for the Pike's Peak library, which serves special interest groups including children and minority groups, all other reported library systems are generic in the nature of their I&R services.

As shown in Table 8-3, the seven libraries under study were established between 1972 and 1977. According to the general findings of the national library survey reported by Childers (1984), half of all library-based I&R programs were started within the four-year period 1975–1978, thus pointing to the recency and rapidity of I&R developments in public libraries. The service areas within which library-based I&R services operate are primarily local. Almost 86% of the I&R libraries serve the limited area of either a city, town, school district, or single county. In con-

TABLE 8-3 Selected Library-Based I&R Programs by Location, Year Established, Service Area, Population, Budget, and Outside Funding Sources

Library-Based I&R Programs	Location	Year Established	Service Area	Population	Budget	Outside Funding Sources
APL/CAT (A Programming Language/Community Access Tool)	Dallas, Texas	1972	county and city	940,000	$65,000	city planning council
LINC (Library Information Center)	Memphis, Tennessee	1974	4 counties & neighborhood communities in Arkansas & Mississippi	900,000	$30,000 (1981)	revenue sharing, city funds, AAA
AID (Accurate Information Desk)	Baltimore County, Maryland	1974	county (excluding Baltimore)	717,734	$83,500	LSCA
CIP (Computerized Community Information Project)	San Mateo, California	1972	county (19 incorporated cities)	582,200	$69,119	LSCA, county, revenue sharing, Title III (OAA)

*CALL (Citizens Action Line Limitless)	Pike's Peak, Colorado Springs, Colorado	1977	county and city	322,000	$75,000	CETA
DIS (Direct Information Service)	Amherst, Massachusetts	1972	2 counties	153,000	$38,200 (1980)	LSCA, county gvt., directory sales, United Way
I&R	Caroline County, Maryland	1975	1 county	23,400	$23,000	LSCA

*Other files on-line: COURSES, CLUBS, CALENDAR, DAY CARE

Source: Childers, T. (1984). *Information and referral: Public libraries.* Norwood, NJ: Ablex Publishing Corporation.

trast, the reported I&R model systems tend to represent larger service areas, including multicounty and statewide areas. The selected libraries serve varying populations that range from 940,000 in Dallas to 23,400 in Caroline County, Maryland. As indicated in Table 8-4, the service areas with the largest population areas do not necessarily report the highest budgetary allocation for I&R operations. In comparing rank order, it is interesting to note that while Dallas ranks highest in population, it ranks fifth of the seven libraries in terms of the amount of money invested in I&R operations. Not surprisingly, the Memphis I&R system ranked highest in I&R budget allocation and second in size of service area. While I&R library programs in Caroline County and Pike's Peak ranked second and third in budgetary allocation, they ranked third and fifth in the size of their service areas. The San Mateo County library ranked fourth both in total population and budget allocation. The Amherst and Caroline County libraries ranked lowest (in sixth and seventh place) in total population and budget costs.

RELEVANT STRATEGIES FOR I&R NETWORKING

Given the enormous variations that exist within and between I&R networks, it is important to consider some of the strategies and

TABLE 8-4 Ranking of Library-Based I&R Programs by Population and Budget Allocation

Site of Library-Based I&R	Rank by Total Population Within Service Areas	Rank by I&R Budget Allocation
Dallas, Texas	1	5
Memphis, Tennessee	2	1
Baltimore County, Maryland	3	2
San Mateo County, California	4	4
Pike's Peak, Colorado	5	3
Amherst, Massachusetts	6	6
Caroline County, Maryland	7	7

Source: Childers, T. (1984). *Information and referral: Public libraries.* Norwood, NJ: Ablex Publishing Corporation.

tactics that promote networking and interorganizational coordination. At any given time, the degree of networking may depend upon staff leadership and the readiness of agencies to enter into a mutually agreeable level of association. The strength of the association may depend upon the particular stage of development of the I&R program or pressure from internal or external forces to bring about coordinated I&R programs. For example, the Information Center of Hampton Roads in Virgina, which represents a regional planning area, assumed leadership in the evolution of a statewide I&R network system after demonstrating strong initiative and the competence of its own regional I&R system, which had developed over a 20-year period (1965–1985). In the library system at Amherst, Massachusetts, a public demand for a *Women's Guide* paved the way for the generic I&R program. In Caroline County, Maryland, the state planning department requested that the library develop I&R services.

Degrees of interorganizational coordination vary and range from a climate of informal cooperation, typical of the Denver I&R program, to the formal centralized LINC system that operates in the Memphis library system. Based on the strength of interagency cooperation and coordination of specialized and generic I&R programs, the I&R network that evolved in Los Angeles has developed into an I&R federation. The bi-county I&R system in California's Humboldt and Del Norte counties is the result of a merger of the two separate county systems through joint funding controlled by the local Area Agency on Aging (AAA). The levels and patterns of interorganizational coordination depend upon a host of determinants that may go beyond fiscal support to reflect the unique history and sociocultural characteristics of the community. In Denver, for example, coordination among I&R programs has usually been informal, whereas in Memphis the LINC program has, from the outset, maintained formal interorganizational relationships.

The direction of coordination may follow a top-down or bottom-up approach. National organizations in the public and voluntary sectors tend to follow the top-down approach. In carrying out coordinated I&R programs, as specified in the 1974 amendments of the Older Americans Act, the three-tiered administrative structure of the national Administration on Aging (AoA), which includes State Units on Aging (SUAs) and local Area Agencies on Aging (AAAs), has promoted coordination at all these hierarchical levels (see Appendix A). In the voluntary sector, the American Red Cross has developed I&R programs at its national headquarters and, in a top-down approach, has encouraged local Red Cross chapters to implement I&R programs in collaboration with other existing I&R agencies (Tannenbaum, 1981). Conversely, the networking process may start from the bottom and proceed up. For example, the Information Center of Hampton Roads in Virginia began in 1965 as a specialized health I&R center, then developed a broad generic base, which in 1982 also incorporated specialized services to the aged and the disabled. The public library in Dallas began a small card file of community services in 1970 that mushroomed into an extensive clearinghouse for all information and/or referral agencies in the Greater Dallas Area.

Experience has indicated that the success of interorganizational networking depends upon various strategies that promote effective interagency relationships. The critical factor is the extent to which networking can benefit the individual member agency yet promote the mutual interests of all the members of or participants in interorganizational networks. Given the broad

---

TABLE 8-5 Strategies for I&R Networking

Organizational Strategies

- Interorganizational mandates, contracts, and agreements
- Location and co-location of I&R programs
- Staffing and training
- Multiple funding/joint financing
- Outreach and public relations

Service Strategies

- Centralized resource inventories
- Linkages of generic and specialized I&R services
- Collaborative and complementary services
- Adherence to I&R standards

Policy and Planning Strategies

- Political support
- Joint research and evaluation
- Intra-agency and interagency planning

---

variations that exist within and between I&R networks, an examination of some of the strategies and tactics that create effective linkages merits further analysis. As shown in Table 8-5, networking strategies are analyzed according to organizational strategies (structural) and service strategies (functional). A third category, policy and planning strategies, includes legislative activities, evaluation, and research. A review of different strategies that promote I&R networking is based primarily on the reports of the model systems study (Shanahan et al., 1983) and the library-based I&R survey (Childers, 1984).

Organizational Strategies

As previously noted, the Administration on Aging is the only federal agency that mandates I&R services through coordinated networks of I&R programs that operate on federal, state, regional, and local levels. To promote networks that will implement I&R programs at each of the hierarchical levels, the AoA has organized the federal I&R Consortium, representing both public and private agencies. The major purpose of the consortium is to foster linkages at all levels of I&R programming and to promote coordination of I&R systems within networks through formal contracts and informal agreements. The strategy of working agreements between the AoA and each of the representative federal agencies has promoted interagency coordination on the federal level, with the understanding that each of these federal agencies will coordinate I&R developments in their respective state, regional, and local offices.

The LINC network is a unique model of an autonomous I&R system that is located within the central public library and serves the I&R needs of the library, but also functions simultaneously as an interagency network. While LINC operates with its own staff and budget as a separate entity within the library, this I&R system also carries out the library's priority role as a comprehensive information center for all residents of the service area. LINC conducts joint projects with voluntary social agencies as well as with public agencies, including the public health and the police departments.

Staff training can also be effective in promoting cooperation and coordination. Multiple I&R agencies can collaborate in preparing educational materials and conducting training programs through seminars, institutes, and workshops, as reported in the training programs conducted by staff of the Los Angeles I&R Federation. Staff trainers from the Information Center of Hampton Roads in Norfolk, Virginia, provide technical assistance and training in the operation of their on-line I&R information system to their own agency staff and to staff agencies involved in their I&R system. In Memphis, the LINC system provides an interesting example of cross-training of I&R staff and library reference personnel. This joint training program is exceedingly effective, since I&R and reference services may overlap or even conflict. In the Caroline County Public Library in Maryland, I&R is integrated into the regular reference department (Childers, 1984).

A highly effective strategy to advance coordination is the judicious sharing of funds in carrying out joint programs. For example, a cooperative venture to enhance coordination is the federal support of the Humboldt and Del Norte counties I&R system in northern California. In the voluntary sector, the United Way of America has strongly promoted networking through financial support of interagency collaboration in the Mile High I&R system in Denver. Private subsidization of automated I&R programs by business corporations has been a prime factor in expanding interagency networks in Phoenix and in Seattle (Garrett, 1984). Some networks operate through a funding pattern that involves a voucher or franchise system. A franchise plan for coordinated networks was proposed by Long (1974) whereby a centralized I&R system offers payment to local I&R service agencies to carry out the direct service tasks in accordance with standards of quality service defined by the central I&R unit. Conversely, a pattern of coordination that requires payment from the local I&R agency to the central I&R unit has proved feasible in Monroe County, New York, where the central public library I&R system receives payment from individual agencies for the purchase of a centralized county directory and the handling and dissemination of aggregated data reports. Funding from various public and voluntary sources has generated organizational networking, as apparent in the multifunding pattern of the Los Angeles I&R

Federation, the Connecticut Info-Line and in the library-based I&R system in Amherst, Massachusetts.

Joint efforts at outreach and public relations can usually generate far greater interest than single agency efforts can accomplish. For example, Connecticut's Info-Line gained political support and a stronger fiscal base of operation when it linked its computerized resource data system with the department of social services. In Memphis, the library's cable television channel is used to disseminate service information about LINC. Public service announcements are distributed to radio and televion stations, and LINC posters appear on buses. Important features of the Dallas Public Library publicity campaign are direct mailings to corporations with employee assistance programs and published announcements to motels and hotels that cater to professional organizations.

Service Strategies

One of the major benefits of I&R networking is the sharing of a centralized resource inventory that can be used by member agencies for purposes of resource identification, retrieval, and reliable updating. Whether manual or automated, the resource file provides networking capabilities through the use of a uniform service classification system available to all member agencies of the I&R network. A case in point is the development of the first computer-ready resource directory for New York City, produced through the collaboration of the Community Council of Greater New York, the New York City Department of Human Resources Administration, and the United Way/Greater New York Fund. Another example of effective and comprehensive networking through a shared resource file is the Computerized Resource Inventory (CRI) that the Info-Line of Connecticut developed with the participation of staff from regional I&R offices. Utilizing the central resource files in Hartford, mailing labels, special reports for funders and planners, and regional editions of the *Info-Line Directory of Community Services* are produced for each region.

Networking also bridges generic and specialized service to pro-

vide more comprehensive services to the consumer, as evident in
the program of the Information Center of Hampton Roads
(ICHR), which has combined services for the aged and the handicapped within a comprehensive generic system. Another example is the I&R Federation in Los Angeles, which offers training
opportunities and technical assistance to the American Heart
Association. By sharing skills and staff competencies, I&R networking can promote economy as well as service effectiveness.
Info-Line in Connecticut and the ICHR in Virginia promote networking for various social agencies through initial screening of
clients at service entry and by providing needed follow-up services. To promote quality services, I&R networks can exercise
some measure of control by insisting on compliance to standards
of performance in I&R service delivery. To promote a coordinated I&R network within the Humboldt and Del Norte
County area in northern California, compliance with defined
standards was required by the Area Agency on Aging (AAA) as a
condition for continued funding.

Co-location of I&R services at one-stop, multi-agency service
centers can promote I&R networking, providing the member
agencies do not operate independently or competitively but
rather function as a coordinated network with clearly defined interagency linkages. An example of a strategic location for I&R
that promotes coordination is the centralized operation of the
I&R Tie-Line in North Dakota, which is located in the governor's office.

Policy, Planning, and Research Strategies

Opportunities for joint planning and policy formulation have
gained increased recognition as interagency data are shared for
policy and planning purposes. Networking may occur not merely
as a result of planning but, in fact, as a precondition for planning,
as occurred in the I&R systems that developed in Los Angeles,
Connecticut, and metropolitan Denver. However, it should be
noted that networking may also occur serendipitously without
prior planning. An example is the LINC program in Memphis,
which was initiated when an unexpected sum of $1 million was
released under a federal revenue-sharing grant. An observer of

I&R networking notes that "it is not necessary to wait for the favorable political climate and funding necessary for a formalized network, and perhaps it is not even desirable to do so. Cooperative arrangements result from interpersonal relationships, leadership styles, timing and even serendipity, as often as they do out of purposeful planning" (Dehner, 1979, p. 27).

Since the 1970s, networking for the purpose of planning has been increasingly recognized by I&R operators and analysts. The determination of "best practice" that was made in the selected I&R model networks is based upon planful cooperation and coordination by each of these model systems. Not only do I&R agencies provide a data base for planning by the I&R agencies, but outside agencies, groups, and organizations also use I&R data bases for research, evaluation, and planning. LINC reported a vast array of requests for information, research, and planning from outside groups and agencies, including the Federal Information Center, statewide training workshops, Memphis State University, and many voluntary, fraternal, and civic organizations (Shanahan, Gargan & Apple, 1983, pp. 96–97).

NETWORKING: AN ASSESSMENT

In the absence of a central national policy, I&R has developed sporadically, with wasteful duplications and unfilled gaps in service provision. In most American communities a formal I&R network does not exist, and trying to develop a network within uncoordinated systems of human services is a difficult and complex task. What appears to be an integrated plan for I&R service delivery may be no more than a clustering of agencies that remain autonomous and discrete. It is also possible for an I&R organization that operates in relative isolation to develop into another specialized service, thereby contributing to the general fragmentation of services. Furthermore, duplication of services may stem from the categorical nature of federal funding and the lack of coordination among funding agencies whose concerns are not limited to the operations of an I&R agency or any single service program. Taking a critical view of the lack of coordinated networking in I&R developments, Glaser (1979) observed that "the uncontrolled proliferation and lack of coordination makes a mockery of the very thing we're in business to do. In too many of our communities I&R has sadly become a part of the problem and not its solution."

However, despite the benefits of coordination, it is a goal that is often difficult to achieve, and even more difficult to sustain, because of agency autonomy, turf problems, and competition among interest groups to attract constituencies and obtain resources. By continuing to respond to the interests of specialized groups and by receiving insufficient funds for programs earmarked for coordinated activities in the planning and delivery of human services, I&R has waged an uphill struggle during the past 25 years in its efforts to promote more integrated human services.

From another point of view, it has been argued that coordination may not necessarily be a desirable goal. A degree of duplication may be intentional since it can provide consumer choices and service alternatives by offering a variety of convenient and acceptable entries to services. Taking a balanced view, Perrow (1978) points out that "coordination has costs associated with it, as well as presumed benefits, and that there may be substantial gains with redundant, uncoordinated activity and substantial costs with concentration which eliminates back-up facilities." Experience indicates that a neatly integrated human service system may not be possible to establish in the United States. The traditional American suspicion of centralized authority in the delivery of human services may work against the apparent desirability of increased networking.

Despite the apparent limitations and constraints in creating comprehensive centralized I&R networks within the American social welfare system, the process of what has been called "facilitative I&R networking" is continuing to prove effective. According to Austin (1980), facilitative networks denote viable and flexible community service systems that accommodate to a society of continuing change and limited resources. Given the demonstrated level of I&R development to date and the potential of an expanding information technology, a futuristic perspective on I&R is ventured in the concluding chapter.

IV Conclusions and Projections

9   I&R Megatrends: A Prospective View

"The most reliable way to anticipate the future is by understanding the present."
—John Naisbitt, *Megatrends: The New Directions Transforming Our Lives*

I&R is essentially a very recent social service phenomenon. It has been observed that "despite its relatively short history as a public policy, I&R has achieved a central role in the social services. The rate of diffusion and adoption of I&R activities has been more rapid than for most innovations" (Shanahan, Gargan, & Apple, 1983, p. 208). Although the roots of I&R have been traced to the social service exchanges of a century ago, I&R, as an identifiable and distinguishable organized service, is essentially a product of the 1960s. The state of the art in I&R is embryonic and uneven.

185

Much of what is currently done in I&R is based on acknowledgment of its merit rather than systematic study and tested demonstration of its efficiency and effectiveness. Since there has been a paucity of research reports and evaluative studies in I&R operations, there is an inherent danger of locking future systems into modes of operation that are essentially untested. Therefore, in order to maximize the capabilities of I&R as responsive and responsible organized access systems in a rapidly changing society, a prospective view of I&R developments in the light of present and projected trends can suggest new directions and new challenges.

A FUTURISTIC VIEW ON I&R

It is expected that I&R will forge ahead in new directions and will strive to achieve its potential as an effective entry system to human services. A consideration of some of the major trends, or "megatrends" (Naisbitt's term), may contribute to an appreciation of the present state of the art with a view toward the future. It is suggested that the following ten megatrends will, in varying ways, continue to shape the course of I&R developments. There is no weighting of importance assigned in the listing below; it is assumed that each of these trends, either singly or, more likely, in combination, will impact upon the continued development of I&R in the United States.

1. Unplanned access to services⟷Planned access to service systems
2. High tech for I&R⟷High touch through I&R
3. Client assisted I&R services⟷User self-help services
4. Specialized I&R programs⟷Generic I&R programs
5. I&R in traditional settings⟷I&R in nontraditional settings
6. I&R organizational systems⟷Interorganizational I&R networks
7. Microlevel I&R systems⟷Macrolevel I&R systems
8. Undefined staff roles/general tasks⟷Delineated staff/roles specific tasks

9. Direct I&R service programs◄─────►Policy, planning, and
   research in I&R
10. Access systems in the United States◄─────►Access systems abroad

Unplanned Access to Services◄─────►Planned Access
to Service Systems

The profusion of services in the American social welfare system
that began in the 1930s and accelerated in the 1960s has occurred in reaction to changing socioeconomic conditions and
political pressures. Consumer demands and special interests have
also exerted varying influences on the course of American social
welfare at different times and for different reasons. The consequences of this lack of planning is the existing maze of fragmented, uncoordinated services that provide inadequate access
to social services and social programs.

I&R systems will continue to expand with inevitable diversity
but with increased planfulness and accountability. Diminished
public funding and service retrenchments have brought about
new organizational alliances and professional collaborations in
the development of broader I&R networks, not only in the public
and voluntary sectors, but also increasingly in the proprietary
(for-profit) sector. The trend toward I&R expansion under private auspices is already evident in the growth of management
funded employment assistance programs (EAPs) and corporate
supported resource and referral (R&R) programs for child day
care (see Chapter 2). I&R development in the private sector may
continue to expand as I&R is recognized as an effective and efficient way to facilitate access to needed services and as fee-for-
service payments become an acceptable practice. An inherent
danger in fee-for-service is that I&R may abandon its universal
commitment to serve all inquirers and become available only to
those who can afford to pay.

Broader application of information technology and the adap-
tive growth of information systems will continue to be major
catalysts in the development of centralized data banks for social
planning. However, systematized entries to services do not imply
creation of a planned society. The goal of I&R is not to establish

blueprints of service systems but to bridge some of the gaps and overcome the persistent barriers that impede the routes to needed services, benefits, and entitlements. Austin (1980) refers to I&R as "the new glue for the social services" which can provide cohesion through "facilitative networking." Long (1973a, p. 60) assigns a more dynamic role to I&R as a force for change, forecasting that "from an historical point of view, I&R centers may be only a transitional step toward a centralized assessment and referral service for all human services." While the extent to which I&R may be able to impact upon the basic infrastructure of American social welfare remains uncertain, the potential of I&R suggests improved access to services.

High Tech for I&R ←—→ High Touch Through I&R

The information age has been brought about by a rapidly advancing high technology that has impacted all aspects of society, including the organization and delivery of human services. In the field of information and referral services, high technology is replacing the obsolete shoebox files, timeworn catalogue cards, and outdated directories. Organized data systems are producing more effective information management, promoting efficient information retrieval, and providing access to multiple interactive data systems. As high technology has continued to advance, the indispensable human relations aspects and interpersonal relationships (called "high touch" by Naisbitt) have gained increased importance. The provision of the human dimension is necessary to offset possible depersonalization and alienation between providers and consumers in a high-tech society. I&R is, in a sense, a social invention to counteract the possible evils inherent in a "digital society" (Vallee's term, 1982).

Attention to human values in information services and referral is essentially what I&R is about. In the delivery of I&R services, information assistance, referral processing, and follow-up activities are basically human relations tasks. Spurred by technological advances that promote its availability and accessibility, information will be shared with many more in many more places. The opportunities for more openness in decision making and policy formulation are made possible by the "informization" brought about by high technologies (Cleveland, 1985).

I&R workers are professional caretakers and trained human service helpers. I&R services, which range from information assistance to referral, follow-up, and advocacy, offer help that goes beyond a reference file or a computer printout. If I&R is viewed as an open doorway to services, there can be no "closed doors" and therefore no "closed cases" in I&R operations. The universal entry to I&R is intended to remain open and available to all inquirers to "come to" and "return to" as need or circumstance may indicate.

While Kahn (1970, p. 96) viewed access services as an important redistributive strategy, he conceded that I&R is not a social equalizer; it can neither reach all who are in need nor be distributed in accordance with a rational priority system. Nevertheless, I&R is a social utility that is designed as a "first call for help." Because of its ability to respond to all inquiries with professional promptness and to avoid delays whenever possible, I&R can perform a preventive function by meeting some of the anticipated needs of individuals and families before more perilous problems occur (primary prevention). If possible, amelioration or reduction of a given problem (secondary prevention) can be achieved. Another preventive goal for an I&R service is the treatment or management of an acknowledged problem through appropriate and timely intervention (tertiary prevention).

Client Assisted I&R Services ←——→ User Self-Help Services

As automated information systems are used more extensively, computerized services are increasingly designed to be user-friendly, thus further increasing their use. Information seekers are able to avail themselves of information resources that they can operate independently or with minimal assistance. Unlike traditional I&R services, which assumed that every inquiry required a staff response, future I&R services will be more available, accessible, and manageable for the user. Analagous to the book-borrowing patron of the public library, who independently selects books and other published materials, the information seeker will possess, or quite readily acquire, the ability to retrieve data and extract information from data systems quite independently. As more information becomes available through the use of home-based computerized equipment, including interactive videotex and cable, the I&R end-user will have unprecedented opportunities for self-help.

Information bases will be conveniently available for the direct I&R user at such strategic locations as local libraries, neighborhood schools, train stations, community hospitals, town halls, shopping plazas, and churches. Intersystem communication among I&R programs in diversified settings will provide exchanges of many different kinds of data systems that can be monitored on-line through the use of terminals. Reduced costs of computer hardware and the development of less complex and more adaptable software will significantly expand the consumer's utilization of automation in I&R operations.

Specialized I&R Programs⟷Generic I&R Programs

The early development of I&R parallels the development of the social welfare movement, which favored the provision of specialized services in such categories as mental health, chronic illness, and aging. Although these early I&R programs focused on specialized services, the need for access to generic I&R services is seen as a basic requirement for adequate I&R provision. To justify the claim that it fosters comprehensive social welfare services, I&R must be prepared to serve or direct callers to generic as well as specialized bodies of information. In promoting optimal utilization of available information, program operators are often faced with decisions on how comprehensive an I&R program should be in providing services to all inquirers. On the other hand, how specialized should an I&R be to serve the particular interests of population groups in need of access to specific services? While specialization often has fundraising appeal and may provide needed expertise for specific population groups, the boundaries of social problems exceed the limits of any single information system and therefore require generic bases with effective linkages to specialized data sources. The goal of I&R operations is to facilitate easy access and interchange between general and specialized I&R information sources, depending on the nature of the inquiry and the resources available. As networks of data bases become more readily available, systematized access to either specialized or generic information bases can be facilitated.

I&R in Traditional Settings ⟷ I&R in Nontraditional Settings

Although I&R is often viewed as an integral service component of organized social agencies, it is also increasingly recognized as a distinct service modality. Since there is no single point of entry that serves all inquirers, I&R must meet the convenience and preferences of consumers and not be restricted to the traditional social agency setting. Centralized data banks will enable inquirers to procure information on human services through computer operations, advanced telephone communications, cable, and interactive videotex at home, in offices, and in libraries. Access points for decentralized I&R service delivery must logically be available at locations where people tend to congregate, for example, shopping plazas, train stations, churches, city halls, and recreation centers.

The trend toward establishing I&R services in community-based institutions (e.g., in libraries, schools, and hospitals) to enhance and promote the major function of the institution has already been demonstrated. The library is an especially suitable locus for I&R operations because of its highly respected position in the community, universal entry, ready accessibility for community residents, and convenient hours of operation, which exceed those of most social agencies. Moreover, the public library is the repository of informational materials and provides the professional skills for information storage and retrieval.

As seen in union counseling programs and the more recent employment assistance programs, I&R in the work place has gained prominence and will continue to expand as more social welfare programs are institutionalized in industry for the mutual benefit of employees and company management.

I&R Organizational Systems◄───►Interorganizational I&R Networks

The traditional mode for I&R service delivery has been for an individual agency to provide an I&R program tailored to its own interests and priorities. However, the growing need for access to central information centers that are capable of systematically maintaining updated files on available resources has prompted the single, independent I&R agency to link up with available centralized I&R bases when possible. I&R agencies are finding it increasingly necessary to enter into partnerships and alliances and become members of networks of I&R service systems. Patterns of I&R networking vary according to the readiness of agencies to share data and participate in centralized functions through alliances that can prove mutually beneficial for all member organizations within viable service networks.

Professional skills and expertise are required to develop and maintain interorganizational relationships that can serve the interests of each member agency and the collective entity. Joint funding arrangements, shared tasks, combined training programs, computer time sharing, and pooled data inventories for research and planning are all centralized functions that can be provided through coordinated interorganizational networks of multiple I&R systems. Problems of organizational turf and issues of confidentiality will inevitably surface and will need to be handled by well-trained, competent staff.

Microlevel I&R Systems◄───►Macrolevel I&R Systems

I&R has historically developed as locality-specific community programs, operationally restricted to the confines of a circumscribed service area, and operative as a horizontal microlevel system. Because the local community is the critical level of entry, I&R will continue to focus on the local level while seeking linkages with state, regional, and national levels of I&R operations. Over the past 25 years, I&R programs have expanded beyond the neighborhood level and are tending to function vertically as macrolevel I&R systems on all hierarchical levels including local, regional, state, and national levels.

Since the 1960s and early 1970s, the funding support at the

federal level has provided initiatives for innovation and experimentation in I&R program developments and research studies. The federal role will continue to be a guiding force for policy, programming, and research. The regional level offers opportunities for expansion within viable and flexible service parameters that go beyond restrictive jurisdictional boundaries. On the state level, the Title XX funds that promoted the rapid expansion of I&R programs in the 1970s have been sharply curtailed and incorporated in the omnibus legislation of 1981 that relies on funds from social services block grants (SSBGs). In competing for these state grants, political sophistication and attention to sound research in I&R program developments are essential to demonstrate the efficacy of I&R in providing improved access to available services. Experience has indicated that state-level I&R operations can also serve as the guardian of standards for I&R practice and the base for centralized service classifications and uniform reporting procedures.

In view of the complexities of the American social welfare system, the trend is to extend I&R service delivery capabilities beyond the boundaries of a single (microlevel) system by meshing and coordinating services with relevant systems at other levels (macrolevel), thereby creating diverse patterns of I&R operations.

Undefined Staff Roles/General Tasks◄───►Delineated Staff Roles/Specific Tasks

In the development of I&R, the roles and tasks of professionals, paraprofessionals, and volunteers have often been blurred and only vaguely defined. Delineation of staff functions will gain clarity as job descriptions include greater specificity of job tasks. It has become apparent that the expertise required for effective I&R operations entails a professionalism that combines competence in direct client services with skills in administration, policy making, staff training, and planning. The tasks of paraprofessionals and volunteers will continue to center around direct service delivery but will expand to include outreach, public relations, and advocacy. The expansion of a corps of well-informed and adequately trained volunteers will become increasingly important, given the anticipated increased demand for I&R services in an era of diminished public funding. I&R staff performance will inevitably depend upon the availability and adequacy of supervision and ongoing training programs. The major sources for volunteer recruitment will continue to be the older, retired citizen, the preprofessional in human services, and the student, including the high school as well as the college and graduate student.

Educational programs in I&R need to impart essential operational and programming skills to the professional I&R generalist. Instruction in information technology and human relations skills must be incorporated into all training programs for human service professionals, appropriately related to staff needs. Ongoing in-service agency programs and on-the-job training programs are essential for agency staff to promote the continued development and refinement of I&R skills. New opportunities for career advancement and greater recognition of professional status for the field of I&R will attract larger numbers of professionals into operating I&R programs.

Direct I&R Service Programs◄──►Policy, Planning and Research Programs in I&R

While direct services to inquirers is the *raison d'être* for I&R programs, greater attention needs to be given to the capacities of I&R to provide current and reliable data for policy formulation, planning, and research. As more I&R programs participate in interactive information systems and planfully link up with multiple data sources, access to information will permit more sharing and pooling of information than has been possible to date.

Research will be significantly enhanced with the availability of central data banks that can be used for exploring a variety of areas for investigation, such as the different effects of alternative modes of access, the incidence and gravity of social problems, client tracking, case management, the effectiveness of service delivery for identified target populations, and comparative strategies for interorganizational linkages. On a note of caution, it should not be presumed that I&R, in and of itself, has the capabilities of overcoming existing gaps and inadequacies in needed services. Clearly, I&R, as a single social service modality, cannot solve the broad societal problems of poverty, unemployment, and discrimination.

I&R can, however, serve as a barometer to spot trends, identify needs and gaps, and reflect changing priorities. While I&R tends to be responsive and reactive, it can also assume a proactive role by indicating new directions for service delivery based on empirical data derived from the compilation of I&R service statistics. The extent to which I&R may be able to reconceptualize or in any way reshape the social welfare system will clearly depend upon the extent of political endorsement and fiscal support that it can muster.

Access Systems in the United States ◄──► Access Systems Abroad

Reports on the growing developments of access systems abroad have provided interesting and significant models worthy of study and exploration. In addition to the British CABs, which have been discussed in some depth, new models and hybrids of access systems, uniquely adapted to the specific culture and national ethos of the respective countries, are evolving. Clearly, the transferability of any service system from one country to another runs the risk of replication and precludes duplication because of inherent cross-national differences in cultures and social welfare systems.

Nonetheless, a familiarity with access systems in both developed and developing countries can offer helpful guidelines in creating more effective information and referral services. Among the lessons that have been learned from reports from abroad is the universality of the need for organized access systems and an acknowledgment of the vast diversity that exists in the organization and delivery of these access systems. Whether the focus is on I&R systems in the United States or Canada, or on CAB systems in Great Britain, Australia, India, Israel, or New Zealand, it is clear that access requires a systematized data base, whether manually operated or computerized. The trend toward automation and the application of information technology will continue to advance, though very likely at an uneven pace. In all reported access systems the role of the volunteer as the direct service agent is central to the delivery of access services. Unlike most American I&R services, the British system tends to give greater recognition to the capabilities of CABs to provide essential data for policy, planning, research, and social reform.

Thanks to the wonders of automation and new modes of communication, more instantaneously shared information throughout planet earth and outer space has become available. The rapidity and accessibility of this simultaneously shared information across continents have produced the concept of "a global information society" (Cleveland, 1985). The extent to which I&R can or will function as an organized international service has been minimally explored to date; however, it has been acknowledged that in a world of mobile population groups, cross-national information and referral services may be appropriately used to assist displaced citizens, refugee groups, and newly arrived minorities to find needed resources through organized access systems.

The actual extent to which these megatrends will impact the continued development of I&R services, agencies, and networks is difficult to predict, but it is certain that the political climate will be a critical determinant in I&R developments (Levinson, 1987, p. 919).

POLICY, POLITICS, AND I&R PROVISION

I&R is needed by almost everyone at some time in their lives. Its usefulness in facilitating access to services is readily acknowledged, but the policy of universal access is not without problems, given the infinite range of human needs and the limited resources available. The political realities indicate that in an era of shrinking funds and service retrenchments, the need for I&R may indeed become more crucial and require increased cooperation on the part of service providers. But the benefits of collaboration and networking are stymied by the competition for limited funding. Can I&R receive the necessary budgetary support as long as it is regarded as a "soft" and peripheral service? Will block grants be allocated primarily to the more traditional, visible "hard" services? Is I&R expansion a disguised demand for more services? The I&R experience to date has indicated serious constraints due to limited funds, staffing insufficiencies, inadequate community support, and problems in interorganizational coordination.

The absence of a national policy on I&R reflects its lack of political support. Without the endorsement of legislators, funders, and critical decision makers, I&R can only exert a limited impact on access to services. Taking a long-range perspective, can I&R be conceived as a transitional step toward a possible central assessment of all human services? Before making any projections, however, I&R needs to be examined within the context of policy issues that may determine the future scope and patterns of the spectrum of human services. Will doorways to human services be open to all inquirers as a universal right and entitlement? Will population groups that are in greatest need of I&R be served? Who will make that determination? How can "information equity" be secured for all socioeconomic groups? Since access to information means access to power, who will control the right to access?

Endowed with a basic adaptability to changing conditions, sensitive to shifting priorities, and responsive to legislative mandates, I&R systems have demonstrated their capacity to facilitate access to existing services and to respond to new demands for needed services. However, lest the capabilities of I&R appear to be grossly overstated, Kahn's sobering comment bears mention: "access services are difficult to do well. Nor are they everything. Yet they are highly important—indeed, they are indispensable. They merit attention, experimentation, and support" (Kahn, 1970, p. 101).

Appendixes

Appendix A: Totals of I&R Programs Reported by State According to Selected Sources (1967–1985)

Total I&R Agencies	Area Agencies on Aging 1985*	AIRS 1984†	United Way of America 1985**	Social Service Exchanges 1969‡	Brandeis Study 1967°
Alabama	13	2	7	0	3
Alaska	1	1	0	0	0
Arizona	8	4	3	0	2
Arkansas	8	7	2	1	6
California	33	52	15	1	30
Colorado	15	9	8	0	2
Connecticut	5	8	13	0	6
Delaware	1	2	1	0	3
District of Columbia	1	2	0	0	2
Florida	11	17	16	0	8
Georgia	18	6	7	0	0
Hawaii	4	4	2	0	3
Idaho	6	6	3	0	0
Illinois	13	31	14	1	5
Indiana	16	20	13	1	12
Iowa	13	11	9	2	2
Kansas	11	15	6	0	3
Kentucky	15	4	4	1	9
Louisiana	42	12	4	0	3
Maine	5	2	1	1	6
Maryland	18	20	3	0	5
Massachusetts	23	15	7	1	7
Michigan	14	18	14	2	13
Minnesota	14	9	8	0	4
Mississippi	10	7	7	0	2
Missouri	10	13	7	0	7
Montana	11	3	3	0	1
Nebraska	8	8	2	0	2
Nevada	1	1	2	0	0
New Hampshire	1	7	7	1	0
New Jersey	21	25	17	1	7
New Mexico	4	3	2	0	3
New York	61	45	16	4	40

Total I&R Agencies	Area Agencies on Aging 1985*	AIRS 1984†	United Way of America 1985**	Social Service Exchanges 1969‡	Brandeis Study 1967°
North Carolina	18	11	10	0	3
North Dakota	1	4	1	0	1
Ohio	12	43	31	14	14
Oklahoma	11	7	6	0	6
Oregon	18	12	5	0	0
Pennsylvania	50	32	22	6	5
Rhode Island	1	2	1	1	1
South Carolina	15	2	4	0	4
South Dakota	1	4	2	0	0
Tennessee	9	3	3	0	3
Texas	28	32	24	1	17
Utah	13	10	2	0	1
Vermont	5	2	0	0	0
Virginia	26	12	8	0	5
Washington	13	12	11	0	9
West Virginia	11	4	4	0	2
Wisconsin	6	10	11	1	10
Wyoming	1	4	1	0	1
TOTAL	674	595	369	40	269

Sources:
*A Directory of State and Area Agencies on Aging, 4th ed. (1985, March). State Committee on Aging, House of Representatives, Ninety-ninth Congress. Washington, DC: U.S. Government Printing Office. (Pub. No. 99-490.)
†Alliance of Information and Referral Services, Inc. (1984). Directory of information and referral services in the United States and Canada. Indianapolis: Author.
**United Way 1985 Directory of Information and Referral Services. Alexandria, VA: United Way of America.
‡United Community Funds and Councils of America. (1969) Directory of social service exchanges in the United States and Canada. New York: Author.
°Bloksberg, L., & Caso E.K. (1967). Survey of information and referral services within the United States: Final report. Waltham, MA: Brandeis University, 1967.

Appendix B: Totals of I&R Programs Reported by State According to Regional Areas (1984)

NORTHEAST	TOTAL AGENCIES
Connecticut	8
Delaware	2
Washington, D.C.	2
Indiana	20
Maine	2
Maryland	20
Massachusetts	15
Michigan	18
New Hampshire	7
New Jersey	25
New York	45
Ohio	43
Pennsylvania	32
Rhode Island	2
Vermont	2
TOTAL	243
PERCENTAGE	40.70%

NORTHWEST	TOTAL AGENCIES
Alaska	1
Idaho	6
Montana	3
Oregon	12
Washington	12
Wyoming	4
TOTAL	38
PERCENTAGE	6.3%

SOUTH CENTRAL	TOTAL AGENCIES
Arkansas	7
Louisiana	12
Oklahoma	9
Texas	32
TOTAL	60
PERCENTAGE	10.05%

NORTH CENTRAL	TOTAL AGENCIES
Illinois	31
Iowa	11
Kansas	15
Minnesota	9
Missouri	13
Nebraska	8
North Dakota	4
South Dakota	4
Wisconsin	10
TOTAL	105
PERCENTAGE	17.59%

SOUTHWEST	TOTAL AGENCIES
Arizona	4
California	52
Colorado	9
Hawaii	4
Nevada	1
New Mexico	3
Utah	10
TOTAL	83
PERCENTAGE	13.91%

SOUTHEAST	TOTAL AGENCIES
Alabama	2
Florida	17
Georgia	6
Kentucky	4
Mississippi	7
North Carolina	11
South Carolina	2
Tennessee	3
Virginia	12
West Virginia	4
TOTAL	68
PERCENTAGE	11.40%

Source: Alliance of Information and Referral Services, Inc. (1984). *Directory of information and referral services in the United States and Canada.* Indianapolis, IN: Author.

Appendix C: Summary of National Standards for Information and Referral*

I. OPERATIVE RELATIONSHIPS

The standards included in Section I focus on the responsibilities of the I&R service to the I&R system.

Standard 1: Cooperative Program Development

Each I&R service is a part of an I&R system and should continually develop I&R service programs related to community needs, existing resources, and the activities of other I&R services.

Standard 2: Cooperative Decision Making

Each I&R service should encourage and participate in cooperative planning, implementation of policies, and sustained development of funding sources.

Standard 3: Cooperative Functional Arrangements

Each I&R service should establish and maintain formal and informal cooperative arrangements with other I&R services to minimize duplication and improve service delivery.

Standard 4: Cooperative Administrative Procedures

Each I&R service should use appropriate administrative procedures to implement cooperative arrangements.

*United Way of America (1983). National Standards for Information and Referral Services, pp. 1–2. Alexandria, VA: United Way of America and the Alliance of Information and Referral Systems, Inc.

II. SHARED FUNCTIONS

The standards in Section II describe the functions that should be performed cooperatively within the I&R system.

Standard 5: Classification System

The I&R service should use a classification system based on standard service terminology to facilitate retrieval of service information, to increase the reliability of planning data, to make comparison and evaluation processes consistent and reliable, and to facilitate national comparisons of data.

Standard 6: Resource File

The I&R services should cooperatively develop, maintain, and use an accurate, up-to-date resource file that contains information on available community resources and that produces detailed data on service providers in the area.

Standard 7: Inquirer Data Collection

The I&R service should cooperate with other services to establish and use a system of collecting and organizing inquirer data that meets the needs of both individual inquirers and the whole community.

Standard 8: Data Analysis and Reporting

The I&R service should cooperate with other services to establish and use a method of collecting and organizing data that provides support for community planning activities. This support should consist of statistics, data analysis, and relevant documentation on service use, client characteristics, unmet needs, gaps, and duplications in services.

Standard 9: Training

The I&R service should make training available to paid and volunteer staff.

Standard 10: Promotion

The I&R service should help establish and maintain a planned program of activities to increase community awareness of I&R services and their objectives.

Standard 11: Access to Service

The standards in Section III describe the delivery functions essential for providing information and referral.

III. SERVICE DELIVERY FUNCTIONS

The standards in Section III describe the delivery functions essential for providing information and referral.

Standard 12: Information Giving

The I&R service should provide information about human services to inquirers. This information can range from a limited response (such as an organization's name, telephone number and address) to detailed data about community service systems (such as explaining how a group intake system works for a particular agency), agency policies, and procedures for application.

Standard 13: Referral Giving

The I&R service should provide referral services for inquirers. These consist of assessing the needs of the inquirer, evaluating appropriate resources, indicating organizations capable of meeting those needs, helping callers for whom services are unavailable by locating alternative resources, and actively participating in linking the inquirer to needed services.

Standard 14: Follow-up

I&R services should follow-up referral cases to determine the outcome. Additional assistance in locating or using services may be necessary.

IV. ORGANIZATIONAL STRUCTURE

The standards in Section IV describe the organizational structure under which an I&R service must operate.

Standard 15: Auspices

The auspices under which the I&R service operates should ensure the achievement of I&R goals.

Standard 16: Staff

I&R service staff should be competent, ethical, qualified, and sufficient in number to implement service policies.

Standard 17: Volunteers

The I&R service should involve volunteers to enhance the program's service delivery.

Standard 18: Financing

Financing should be sufficient to provide adequate service and maintain these standards and criteria.

Standard 19: Facilities

I&R services should provide facilities which allow them to operate adequately.

References

Abbott, K. (1970). The importance of information and referral services to older people. In M.B. Holmes & D. Holmes (Eds.), *Handbook of human services for older persons* (pp. 25-48) New York: Human Sciences Press.

Aday, L.A., & Andersen, R. (1975) *Access to medical care.* Ann Arbor: Health Administration Press.

Administration on Aging, Interdepartmental Task Force on Information and Referral, Office of Human Development, Department of Health, Education and Welfare. (1972). *I&R Guide,* Washington, DC: U.S. Government Printing Office (No. 921-730).

Administration on Aging, Office of Human Development, United States Department of Health, Education and Welfare. (1977). *Information and referral services for the elderly.* Washington, DC: U.S. Government Printing Office.

Administration on Aging, Office of Human Development, Department of Health and Human Services. (1984.) *Report of the Consortium on Information and Referral Services.* (Mimeographed report).

AIRS *Newsletter.* (1984, Sept./Oct.). Editorial: Detroit residents vote to [Keep the door open], assure future of local library systems. *XII* (5).

Alliance of Information and Referral Services, Inc. (1974–1979). *Proceedings of the information and referral roundtables.* Phoenix, AZ: Author.

Alliance of Information and Referral Systems, Inc. (1978). *National standards for information and referral services,* Phoenix, AZ: Author.

Alliance of Information and Referral Systems, Inc. (1984). *Directory of informa-*

tion and referral services in the United States and Canada. Indianapolis, IN: Author.

Assistance Group and the Health and Welfare Council of Central Maryland. (1975). *Information and referral training for state units on aging* (AoA Contract).

Austin, D.M. (1980), I&R: The new glue for the social services. *Public Welfare, 38*(4), 38–43.

Bell, D. (1973). *The coming of post-industrial society,* New York: Basic Books.

Bellamy, D.F., & Forgie, D.J. (1984). Impact of advanced technology on I&R in a Canadian provincial context. In R.W. Levinson & K. Haynes, *Accessing human services: International perspectives* (pp. 199-215). Beverly Hills: Sage Publications.

Bloksberg, L.M., & Caso, E.K. (1967). *Survey of information and referral services existing within the United States: Final Report.* Waltham, MA: Brandeis University, Florence Heller Graduate School of Advanced Studies in Social Welfare.

Bolch, E., Long, N., & Dewey, J. (1972). *Information and referral services: An annotated bibliography.* Minneapolis: Institute for Interdisciplinary Studies.

Bowers, G.E., & Bowers, M.R. (1977). *Client information systems* (DHEW Pub. No. 05-76-130). Washington, DC: Human Resource Administration, Department of HEW.

Brasnett, M.E. (1964). *The story of the Citizens Advice Bureaux.* London: The National Council of Social Service.

Braverman, M. (Ed.). (1976). Information and referral services in the public library [Special issue]. *Drexel Library Quarterly, 12* (1 and 2).

Brody, E.M. (1977) Aging. In *Encyclopedia of social work* (Vol. I) (pp. 55–77). Washington, DC: National Association of Social Workers.

Brooke, R. (1972) *Information and advice services,* (Occasional Papers on Social Administration No. 46). London: G. Bell and Sons.

Bruck, L. (1978). *Access—The guide to a better life for disabled Americans.* New York: Random House. David Obst Books.

Bucaro, T.A. (1980). *A study of I&R services for the urban elderly: An exploration of the effects of territorial decentralization.* Unpublished doctoral dissertation, Adelphi University, School of Social Work, Garden City, NY.

Catalogue of Human Services Information Resources Organizations. (1980). Rockville, MD: Project Share.

Cauffman, J.G. (1980). *SEARCH glossary of human problems and services (medical and social),* Vol. II. Los Angeles: Caligraphics.

Childers, T. (1975). *The information poor in America.* Metuchen, NJ: Scarecrow Press.

Childers, T. (1984). *Information and referral: Public libraries.* Norwood, NJ: Ablex Publishing Corporation.

Cleveland, H. (1985). The twilight of hierarchy: Speculations on the global information society. *Information and Referral: The Journal of the Alliance of Information and Referral Systems, 7*(1), 1–31.

Coleman, J., Levinson, R.W., & Braverman, M. (1979). *Directory of resources.* Phoenix: Information and Referral Services, Inc.

Collins, A.H., & Pancoast, D.L. (1976). *Natural helping networks: A strategy for prevention.* Washington, DC: National Association of Social Workers.

Community Resources Information Bank (CRIB). (1978). *Services for Women.* Los Angeles, CA: Department of Public Social Services.

Cooper and Company. (1985). *Costs and benefits of information and referral under the older Americans act.* Administration on Aging, Office of Human Development, Department of Health, Education and Welfare. Washington, DC: Department of Health, Education, and Welfare.

Deahl, T.F. (1976). Technology: The CRIS project marrying word processing and computer output microfilm technology to publish a directory of human services. *The Journal of Information and Referral Systems, Inc., 1*(2), 48–57.

Dehner, J.A. (1979), The network concept in information and referral. *Information and Referral: The Journal of the Alliance of Information and Referral Systems, 1*(3), 25–31.

Directory of National Level Information Sources on Handicapped Conditions and Related Services. (1980). Washington, DC: Clearinghouse on the Handicapped, Office of Special Education and Rehabilitation Services. (OHDS-80-22007).

Donohue, J.C. (1976). The public information center project. In M. Kochen & J.D. Donohue (Eds.), *Information for the Community.* Chicago, IL: American Library Association.

Durrance, J.C. (1984). Community information services—An innovation at the beginning of its second decade. *Advances in Librarianship, 13,* 100–123.

Encyclopedia of Social Work. (1977). Washington, DC: National Association of Social Work.

Gaines, E. (1980). Let's return to traditional library service: Facing the failure of social experimentation. *Wilson Library Bulletin, 55,* 50-53.

Gargan, J. (1980). Governmental responses to the problems of complexity: The development of statewide systems. *Information and Referral: The Journal of the Alliance of Information and Referral Systems, 2*(1), 1–18.

Garner, M.R., & Haynes, K.S. (1980). Statewide information and referral: A conceptual mode. *Information and Referral: The Journal of the Alliance of Information and Referral Systems, II*(283), 22–36.

Garrett, W. (1984). Technological advances in I&R: An American report. In R.W. Levinson & K.S. Haynes (Eds.), *Accessing human services: International perspectives* (pp. 171–198). Beverly Hills: Sage Publications.

Geiss, G.R., & Viswanathan, N. (1986). *Information technology and helping people.* New York: The Haworth Press.

Gilbert, F.B. (1975), *Information and referral: How to do it. Operating the I&R center* (DHEW Publication No. (OHDS 77-20403) (Vol. IV).

Gilbert, N., & Specht, H. (1974). *Dimensions of social welfare policy.* Englewood Cliffs, NJ: Prentice-Hall.

Gilbert, N., & Specht, H. (Eds.) (1986). *Handbook of the social services.* Englewood Cliffs, NJ: Prentice-Hall.

Glaser, J.S. (1979). A role and direction for information and referral services—
The network concept. *AIRS Newsletter, 7*(2).

Goldenberg, A.C. (1987). *1986 AIRS survey-professional training and education.
Graduate level training programs in I&R.* Unpublished manuscript.

Goodroad, M. (1980). South Dakota Tie Line—Evolution of a rural I&R. *AIRS
Newsletter, 7*(4).

Gotsick, P., Moore, S., Cotner, S., & Flanery, J. (1976). *Information for everyday
survival: What you need and where to get it.* Chicago: The American
Library Association.

Greenspan, B. (1979). Child welfare information systems: A tool for the 1980s?
*Information and Referral: The Journal of the Alliance of Information and
Referral Systems, 1*(3), 53–70.

Hall, A.S. (1974). *The point of entry: A study of client reception in the social services.* London: George Allen and Unwin.

Hall, J., & Tucker, A. (1984). *Rhode Island department of elderly affairs, elderly
abuse program: January 1981 to December 1983.* Providence: Rhode Island
Department of Elderly Affairs.

Hansen, R.E. (1978). *One classification system for information and referral and
for planning.* Paper presented at the National Conference on Social
Welfare, Los Angeles, CA.

Haynes, K.S., & Sallee, A.L. (1976). *Pigeonholing social services: A diagnosis and
assessment.* Occasional Paper. Austin: Center for Social Work Research,
School of Social Work, University of Texas.

Hohenstein, C.L., and Banks, J. (1975). *I&R program configuration: A guide for
statewide planning* (DHEW Pub. No. (OHD) (76-20114). Washington, DC:
United States Department of Health, Education and Welfare.

Holmes, M.B., & Holmes, D. (1979). *Handbook of human services for older persons.* New York: Human Sciences Press.

Huttman, E.D. (1985). *Social services for the elderly.* New York: The Free Press.

Hyde, M.O. (1976). *Hotline.* New York: McGraw-Hill.

Interstudy. (1971). *Notes for managers.* Minneapolis: Institute for Interdisciplinary Studies of the American Rehabilitation Foundation. (ERIC Document Reproduction Service No. ED 055 633)

Interstudy. (1971). *Reaching out.* Minneapolis: Institute for Interdisciplinary
Studies of the American Rehabilitation Foundation. (ERIC Document Reproduction Service No. ED 055 637)

Interstudy. (1971). *A training syllabus.* Minneapolis: Institute for Interdisciplinary Studies of the American Rehabilitation Foundation. (ERIC Document Reproduction Service No. ED 055 632)

Interstudy. (1971). *Information and referral services: Volunteer escort service
(working draft).* Minneapolis: Institute for Interdisciplinary Studies of the
American Rehabilitation Foundation. (ERIC Document Reproduction Service No. ED 055 638)

Interstudy. (1973). *The resource file.* Minneapolis: Institute for Interdisciplinary
Studies of the American Rehabilitation Foundation. [DHEW Pub. No.
(OHD) 75-20111.] (ERIC Document Reproduction Service No. ED
055 634)

Interstudy. (1974). *Information and referral services: Interviewing and information giving*. Minneapolis: Institute for Interdisciplinary Studies of the American Rehabilitation Foundation. (ERIC Document Reproduction Service No. ED 055 635)

Interstudy. (1974). *Information-giving and referral* (working draft, 2nd revision). Minneapolis: Institute for Interdisciplinary Studies of the American Rehabilitation Foundation. Washington, DC: U.S. Department of Health and Human Services, Office of Human Development, Administration on Aging [DHEW Pub. No. (OHD) 75-20112]. (ERIC Document Reproduction Service No. ED 055 636)

Jacobson, A. (1986). Why accreditation? *AIRS Newsletter, XIII*(9), 7-8.

Jones, C.S. (Ed.). (1978). *Public library information and referral services* (pp. 98-110). Syracuse, N.Y.: Gaylord.

Kahn, A.J. (1966). *Neighborhood information centers: A study and some proposals*. New York: Columbia University School of Social Work.

Kahn, A.J. (1969). *Theory and practice of social planning*. New York: Russell Sage Foundation, 1969.

Kahn, A.J. (1970). Perspectives on access to social services. *Social Work, 15*(2), 95-101.

Kochen, M., & Donahue, J. (1976). *Information for the community*. Chicago: American Library Association,

Kopecky, F.J. (1972). Office of Economic Opportunity community centers —A critical analysis. In C.A. Kronus & L. Crowe (Eds.), *Libraries and information centers* (pp. 61-72). Urbana, Il.: Univeristy of Illinois Press.

Kronus, C.A., & Crowe, L. (Eds.) (1972). *Libraries and neighborhood information centers*. Urbana, IL: University of Illinois, Graduate School of Library Science.

Lekis, L. (1980). Using I&R data for planning: The process, problems, and potentials. *Information and Referral: The Journal of the Alliance of Information and Referral Systems, 2*(1) 15-29.

Levinson, R.W. (1979a). An exploratory study of formal and informal linkages to community access systems: A strategy for prevention. (Unpublished manuscript).

Levinson, R.W. (1979b). Towards a human resources information and referral system: Health and social services. *Information and Referral: The Journal of the Alliance of Information and Referral Systems, 1*(1), 51-63.

Levinson, R.W. (1981). Information and referral services. Chapter 1. In N. Gilbert & H. Specht (Eds.), *Handbook of the social services* (pp. 13-34). Englewood Cliffs, NJ: Prentice-Hall.

Levinson, R.W. (1985). Thoughts on I&R . . . Interdisciplinary cooperation needed to advance quality of I&R services. *AIRS Newsletter, XIII* (5), 4,8.

Levinson, R.W. (1987). Information and referral services. (1987). In *Encyclopedia of Social Work* (18th ed.) (Vol.1, pp. 914-919). Silver Spring, MD: National Association of Social Workers.

Levinson, R.W., & Haynes, K.S. (1984). *Accessing human services: International perspectives.* Beverly Hills: Sage Publications.

Licker, P.S. (1983). Building a decision support information system for social services. *Information and Referral: The Journal of the Alliance of Information and Referral Systems,* 5(1), 23–26.

Long, N. (1973a). Information and referral services: A short history and some recommendations. *The Social Service Review,* 47(1), 49–62.

Long, N. (1973b). *Wisconsin information service, an I&R network.* Wisconsin Division on Aging, Department of Health and Social Services. (September 1973).

Long, N. (1974). A model for coordinating services. *Administration in Mental Health,* 2(3), 21–24.

Long, N. (1979). Information and referral services in the 1980s: Where should they go? who should lead? will anyone follow? *Information and Referral: The Journal of the Alliance of Information and Referral Services,* 1 (1),1–24.

Long, N., Anderson, J., Burd, R., Mathis, M.E., & Todd, S.P. (1974). *Information and referral centers: A functional analysis* (3rd ed.) (DHEW Publication No. OHD 75-20235). Minneapolis, MN: Interstudy.

Long, N., Reiner, S., & Zimmerman, S. (1971). *The Role of Advocacy.* Minneapolis, MN: Interstudy.

Long, N., & Yonce, L. (1974). *Information and referral services: Evaluation design for a network demonstration.* Minneapolis, MN: Interstudy.

Luck, C. (1976). Staff training for the information center: Information and referral services in the public library. *Drexel Library Quarterly,* 12 (1+2), 69–80.

Maas, N.L., & DeSantis, M. (1982). Building constituent bases: Support and growth for community information and referral. *Information and Referral: The Journal of the Alliance of Information and Referral Systems,* 7, (1), 42–60.

Mandel, B. (1983). The VD national hotline: "High-Tech" Information and Referral. *Information and Referral: The Journal of the Alliance of Information and Referral Systems,* 5(1), 67–75.

Mathews, M.R., & Fawcett, S.B. (1981). *Matching clients and services: Information and referral.* Beverly Hills: Sage Publications.

McCaslin, R. (1979). Perceived training needs of information and referral providers. *Information and Referrals: The Journal of the Alliance of Information and Referral Systems,* 1(2), 20–28.

McKnight, J. (1980). A nation of clients? *Public Welfare Journal of the American Public Welfare Association,* 38(4), 15–19.

Mickelson, J.S. (1979). I&R: A social worker's perspective. *Information and Referral: The Journal of the Alliance of Information and Referral Systems,* 1 (3), 32–52.

Milio, N. (1975). *The care of health in communities: Access for outcasts.* New York: Macmillan.

Naisbitt, J. (1982). *Megatrends: Ten new directions transforming our lives.* New York: Warner Books.

National Commission on Libraries and Information Science. (1983). *Final Report of the Community Information and Referral Task Force.* Washington, DC: Community Information and Referral Services.

New York State Board of Social Welfare. (1980). *Information and Referral in New York State, Final Report.* Albany, NY: Author.

Penniman, W.D., & Jacob, M.E. (1984). Libraries as communicators of information. In R.E. Rice (Ed.), *The new media communication, research and technology.* (pp. 251–268). Beverly Hills: Sage Publications.

Perrow, C. (1978). *Complex organizations* (2nd ed.). New York: Random House.

Perlis, L. (1978, July). The AFL–CIO community services program: What it is and what it does. *Labor Bulletin.*

Perlow, A.H. (1979). *What have you done for me lately?* New York: Benjamin Company.

Puryear, D. (1982). Early I&R programs in libraries. *Information and Referral: The Journal of the Alliance of Information and Referral Systems, 4*(2), 16– 20.

Rehr, H. (Ed.). (1986). *Access to social health care: Who shall decide what?* Lexington, MA: Ginn Press.

Rehr, H., & Mailick, M. (1981). The patient representative: A facilitator of services in the general hospital. *Information and Referral: The Journal of the Alliance of Information and Referral Systems, 3*(1), 1–19.

Roberts, A.R., & Grau, J.J. (1970). Procedures used in crisis intervention by suicide prevention agencies. *Public Health Reports, 85*(8), 691–697.

Roth, H. (1981). Information and referral services for the handicapped. *Information and Referral: The Journal of the Alliance of Information and Referral Systems, III*(1), 69–75.

St. John, D. (1978). *Overview of Human Services Study. President's Reorganization Project.* Washington, DC: Office of Management and Budget.

Sallee, A.L., & Berg, B. (1983). Day care I&R as a corporate child care option. *Information and Referral: The Journal of the Alliance of Information and Referral Systems, 5*(2), 1–18.

Schoech, D.J. (1982). *Computer use in human services: A guide to information management.* New York: Human Sciences Press.

Schoeps, D.J. (1981). Summary of I&R report, June 1, 1979 to May 31, 1980. Washington, DC: U.S. Veterans Administration (unpublished).

Schroeder, E.J. (1981). Online I&R in your Library: The state of the art. *RQ, 21* (2), 128-134.

Shanahan, J.L., Gargan, J.J. & Apple, N. (1983). *Building model I&R systems: A bridge to the future.* Akron, OH: Alliance of Information and Referral Systems Inc.

Siegel, P. (Ed.). (1984). Childcare information and referral. *National Quarterly, 1*(3).

Sullivan, R.J. (1979). Computerized information and referral: An introduction. *Information and Referral: The Journal of the Alliance of Information and Referral Systems, 1*(3), 13–24.

Tannenbaum, M.A. (1981). I and R in the Red Cross: A collaborative program model. *Information and Referral: The Journal of the Alliance of Information and Referral Systems, 3*(1), 37–47.

Tatara, T. (1979). *Access services in the United States: A resource paper.* Unpublished manuscript.

Technical Notes (1980). *Summaries and characteristics of States' Title XX Social Service Plans for the fiscal year* 1979. U.S. Dept. of Health, Education and Welfare. Prepared by Gloria Kilgore and Gabriel Salmon.

Toffler, A. (1981). *The third wave.* New York: Willam Morrow.

U.S. Bureau of the Census. (1984). *Statistical abstract of the United States, 1984.* Washington, DC: U.S. Government Printing Office.

United States General Accounting Office. (1978). *Information and referral for people needing human services—A complex system that should be improved* (HRD-17-134). Washington, DC: Author.

United Way of America. (1973). *National standards for information and referral services.* Alexandria, VA: Author.

United Way of America. (1976). UWASIS II: Taxonomy of social goals and human service programs. Alexandria, VA: Author.

United Way of America. (1974). *Referral agent program.* Alexandria, VA: Author.

United Way of America. (1975). Information and referral: Where can I go for help? *Community, 50*(1), 8–11.

United Way of America. (1978). *Challenge to United Way information and referral.* Alexandria, VA: Author.

United Way of America. (1979). *Information and referral: Programmed resource and training course.* Alexandria, VA: Author.

United Way of America (1980). *Information and referral: Programmed resource and training course.* Alexandria, VA: Author.

United Way of America. (1983). *National standards for information and referral services.* Alexandria, VA: United Way of America and the Alliance of Information and Referral Systems, Inc.

Vigilante, J.L. (1976). Back to the old neighborhood. *Social Service Review, 50* (2), 194–208.

Wittman, M. (1966). *The feasibility of Citizens Advice Bureaux in American social services.* Unpublished manuscript.

Zimmerman, S. (1977). *The use of information and referral services' data in social planning.* Unpublished doctoral dissertation, University of Minnesota, Minneapolis.

Zucker, M, (1965). Citizens Advice Bureaux: The British Way. *Social Work, 10*(4).

Index